SUCCESSFULLY INTEGRATING TWO BUSINESSES

TO KARIN AND MAARTEN
TO KAREN

WHO ARE OUR BEACONS IN LIFE AND WITH WHOM WE LEARN MORE EVERYDAY

IN MEMORY OF MARJOLEIN, MAARTEN'S LITTLE SISTER

SUCCESSFULLY INTEGRATING TWO BUSINESSES

❖

Hans J. C. Bakker
and
Jeroen W. A. Helmink

Gower

Published by
Gower Publishing Limited
Gower House
Croft Road
Aldershot
Hampshire GU11 3HR
England

Gower
Old Post Road
Brookfield
Vermont 05036
USA

British Library Cataloguing-in-Publication Data
Bakker, J. C.
Successfully integrating two businesses
1.Consolidation and merger of corporations
I.Title II.Helmink, W. A.
658.1'6

ISBN 0 566 08368 X

Library of Congress Card Number: 00-100342

Typeset in Great Britain by Ian Kingston Editorial Services, Nottingham, and printed in Great Britain by MPG Books Ltd, Bodmin, Cornwall.

CONTENTS

❖

LIST OF FIGURES

LIST OF TABLES

INTRODUCTION

SUCCESSFUL MERGERS AND ACQUISITIONS: BALANCED BUSINESS STRATEGY OR MILLION DOLLAR GAMBLE?

The last couple of years have been very interesting for those involved in mergers, acquisitions and internal integration projects. Every year bigger deals have been made, and the total volume of deals reaches new heights year after year.

Logically, one would assume that this has been due to the high success rate of this type of business development. However, as almost every manager knows by now, this is certainly not the case. In fact, the results are distinctly disappointing. Failure rates of 50–80 per cent for these ventures can be found in the growing research literature in this area. The conclusions drawn from these analyses are very often negative: a lot of value was destroyed instead of being created, while high premiums were paid.

With these very low success rates, embarking on a merger, acquisition or internal integration venture seems more like a gamble than an effective and balanced business strategy. The way in which some of these deals are done seems to confirm this suspicion. As one manager said to us: if we need to get approval from the Board for an investment project of, say, US$25 million, we need to go through all kinds of procedures, which take time and require careful consideration not only from the Board, but also from specialists, who all give their views on the plan. We then need to get support from division management to guarantee the proposed investment. Preparing the case usually takes many months. Now think about an acquisition of US$750 million. It turns out that this can be done very quickly, without all the red tape attached to regular investments – within a couple weeks if need be. Now, can you understand this?

M&A IS COMPLEX AND IRRATIONAL

This is only one example that we have come across in our work as consultants interested in what is usually called post-merger or post-acquisition integration. By now we know that performing a merger or integrating an acquired company are among the most complex change processes that a company can attempt. There are many factors that contribute to this complexity, yet complexity as such is not the only explanation.

On looking more closely at this process one quickly finds some intriguing facts. Knowledge about the front end, usually identified as the deal phase, has grown significantly over the last ten years. From this, we know that making the wrong decision about a merger or acquisition will cause tremendous problems in the post-acquisition phase.

Armed with this knowledge, a number of companies have tried to streamline the deal phase – some with a high degree of success, such as General Electric, while many others are still struggling with this. Yes, they have a procedure for handling these deals, but most of the time it does not work. Why not? Because the managers involved in the acquisition are focused on only one outcome: doing the deal (of their life?). Despite due diligence, despite financial analysis, and despite risk analysis, very often decisions seem to be guided by the 'belief' in the 'strategic value' of this acquisition, which will result in a lot of 'synergy'. This emotional commitment seems to threaten the professional managerial decision-making process.

And even when this decision making is handled professionally, there is no guarantee that the desired outcome will be feasible. We often come across the following situation: 'It was an interesting opportunity financially speaking, so it was given to a manager to ensure that the planned benefits would be achieved. And unfortunately, this did not happen'.

In our work we also came across companies that wanted to optimize their organization in Europe and migrated from a country-based organization to a regional one. Here the same issues can be found as in post-merger and post-acquisition integration.

LEARNING WITH EXPERIENCED TOP MANAGERS

Of course, managers are not happy with the bad results achieved by some mergers and acquisitions. Many are eager to do something about it, but what? We are convinced that only a very practical approach will help to improve the success rate.

In order to get a better understanding of what happens in everyday life, we decided to approach a small number of major companies (we chose 15) that were, or had been, engaged in mergers, acquisitions or internal integration projects to participate in our project (see the acknowledgements at the end of this introduction for their names). These companies varied from global players to nationally-based organizations. The research was cross-industry, with the aim of collecting a broad array of experiences. When asked, all companies were most willing to participate, which underlined the importance of our attempt to better understand current practices and develop best practices.

METHOD

In order to understand current practices we used a qualitative approach. From the selected companies, a top manager that had been, or still was, responsible for one or more integration projects was interviewed.

The interviews were semi-structured. A questionnaire was used to structure the meeting, but there was enough flexibility to discuss specific details in depth. This improved the scope and detail of the experiences that are presented in this book. After all the interviews were done, the interview results were analysed.

Each participating company was interviewed about one specific project. We took into account whether the company was involved in a merger, an acquisition or an internal integration project. Figure 1 presents an overview.

From current practices to best practices

It is important to understand that we were not interested in getting a representative sample, but rather experiences from various types of project, from which we (together with the managers involved) could learn about current as well as desired (best) practices.

	Merger	Acquisition	Internal integration	Totals
Business to business	1	3	3	7
Consumer goods	3	2	0	5
Commercial services	0	3	0	3
Totals	4	8	3	15

Figure 1 Overview of types of projects.

Besides personal interviews, interactive sessions were organized with the interviewees in which a number of key findings were presented. Based on the lessons learned and the current practices that we discovered, best practices were developed with the top managers that we interviewed in a brainstorm exercise using a groupware system.

FROM POST-ACQUISITION INTEGRATION TO BUSINESS INTEGRATION

When you listen carefully to experienced managers, it quickly becomes clear that the terms *post-merger integration* and *post-acquisition integration* confuse the issue!

A successful merger, acquisition or internal integration does not start after a deal is made (or decision is taken), but long before that! It starts with the business strategy of a company and the way in which this came about. Whether you are considering an acquisition, a merger or an internal integration, all of these are business ventures driven by (hopefully) a business strategy and all are about combining what until then has been separate.

Therefore we use the term *business integration* to underline that all of these ventures are attempts made by top management to realize their business objectives by combining various organizational entities, whether this is a merger with another company or the combining of two previously separate entities within their own company.

This shift in focus underlines the fact that to achieve a successful merger, acquisition or internal integration, an *integrated approach* is needed to handle all of the aspects involved professionally, starting from the corporate vision.

We first published our Business Integration Approach in 1998, based on our consulting experiences and the growing literature on these issues. Now, armed with the experiences of the managers involved, we have improved our approach. This provides a framework for managing business integration projects while using best practices in this area. Figure 2 shows our upgraded Business Integration Approach.

WHAT THIS BOOK IS AND WHAT IT IS NOT

This book has been written to assist top managers to deal more effectively with business integration, and by doing so to improve the quality and enhance the success of these ventures.

It is not a novel. Nor is it a cookbook type of book, yet it contains guidelines and best practices for handling business integration projects. It is not a

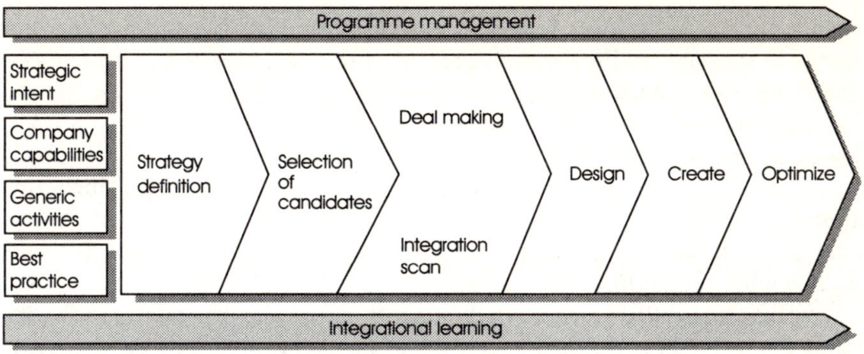

Figure 2 The upgraded Business Integration Approach.

'cookbook' because the complexity of the issue at hand requires tailor-made approaches that recognize the idiosyncrasies of the companies and the people involved. If anything, the book is a reference book for the (top) manager who wants to improve his or her company's track record in business integration using the knowledge gathered by fellow managers and put into a framework by us.

The book starts – *Chapter 1* – with a brief overview of some business integration *cases* that have not brought the benefits that most people expected from them. This is to remind ourselves how difficult these adventures are. It underlines that there are no easily sustainable results in this area. It also contains a more elaborate description of a business integration case to show how, step by step, a project of this type can fail. Chapter 1 helps to keep us humble.

In *Chapter 2* we present our *Business Integration Approach*. This is the framework within which all the experiences and best practices presented here are placed. It also underlines our deeply felt conviction that only with an integrated or holistic approach can real integration success be achieved.

Then we had to make a very difficult choice. Which practices should be presented and how? Keep in mind that every integration project is unique, so many practices could be described. We decided to focus on three major issues and to present each issue in the same way.

Chapter 3 deals with the first issue: *Strategic Decision Making*. The first part of the chapter consists of an overview of how this issue has been handled in a number of integration projects. The second part contains what is now seen by the participating managers as best practice in handling this issue. Finally, the third part contains a framework based on best practices for strategic decision making as part of our Business Integration Approach.

In *Chapter 4* we present the second issue: *Integration Programme Management*. Although it seems obvious, everyday experience shows that this is one of the major stumbling blocks to success. Part I (Current Practices) shows that the scope of planning is in many cases inadequate. Often the objectives do not provide sufficient structure for effective realization. Part II therefore contains a set of best practices. Finally, in Part III we provide a framework for Integration Programme Management.

In *Chapter 5* we address the third issue: *the management of the so-called 'soft side' of business integration.* Here we refer to the management of all people-related issues, such as communication, culture, head count, but also including anxiety, resistance, uncertainty, lack of understanding, insufficient knowledge etc. – in short, those people-related factors that form the majority of the reasons why integration projects fail.

We present real-life practices in this area in Part I. Furthermore, the participating managers have defined a set of best practices for managing the soft side (Part II). Set against this background, we introduce in Part III our framework, called *Integrational Learning*, which links corporate business development with individual growth.

In *Chapter 6* we look again at Integrational Learning from the perspective of *managing for success* in a quickly changing world. Can we change the negative statistics and make business integration more successful? We are convinced – based on all the evidence provided by the participating managers – that this is certainly possible. Yet there is no quick fix in business integration. Those who are looking for that in this book will be disappointed. But those who want to design and implement business integration successfully in their companies will come away with a coherent framework filled with best practices that they can use.

ACKNOWLEDGEMENTS

We would like to thank the following companies and managers for their cooperation in developing this approach. Their contributions about their experiences were very open and honest. The interviews and the interactive sessions were very stimulating and informative.

If, for whatever reasons, practices have been wrongly represented, it is our mistake and not that of the companies which provided these data. Furthermore, the interpretations of the data and the fitting of the best practices into a framework are solely our responsibility. None of the participating companies or their managers can be held responsible for that.

We hope that by building on these experiences, many more companies will be able to get a better grip on their business integration ventures.

Participating companies and executives (in alphabetical order):

Royal Ahold
International Food Retail
Mr J. W. van Boven
VP Mergers & Acquisitions

Albron
Dutch catering
Mrs M. S. H. Fakkert MA
Manager HRM

Ballast Nedam
International construction company
Mr P. M. A. Baaijens MSc
Managing Director

BCD Holdings NV
Multinational group of companies providing business travel management, leisure travel services, travel software solutions and financial services for selected private and institutional investors.
John A. Fentener van Vlissingen
Chairman

Koninklijke Wessanen NV
Mr N. J. M. Kramer
Director Corporate Development

Campina Melkunie
Dairy food company
Mr C. de Ridder LL M
Manager HRM

CR Delta
Producer and global distributor of genetic products and information services
Mr J. Jansen PhD and Mr J. Dommerholt PhD
Executive Board

Delft Instruments
Industrial manufacturing
Mr E. H. de Groot
CEO

Esso/Exxon Benelux
International petrochemical industry
Mr F. T. van Melkebeke
Benelux Human Resources Manager
Mrs C. A. Baker
Training Manager

Pon Holdings
Automotive industry
Mr E. W. Brongersma
CEO

Sdu Publishing
Publishing
Mr S. van Oostrom LL M
Managing Director

Stork NV
Worldwide industrial technology group
Dr E. J. Kaman
Director Corporate Development

Texaco Benelux
International petrochemical industry
Mr A. Vos
Human Resource Director Benelux

Other participants

Some companies and executives preferred to remain anonymous. Among these were an international fast-moving consumer goods company and a European retail company.

Our clients

In recent years we have worked together with a number of clients on business integration projects. We would like to thank them for the trust placed in us and the opportunities created for learning together in the area of business integration.

These experiences have shown the overriding importance of integrated and practical solutions, which were designed and implemented together with our clients. We have seen cases of failed integration. In virtually every case, people factors (as described further on in the book) caused these failures. This motivated us even further to look for a framework that could help.

Student support

We would also like to thank Maarten Postma, in 1998 a student of the Erasmus University in Rotterdam (The Netherlands), who helped us collect the materials for this project. He assisted in interviewing all participants and also helped us prepare the data analysis.

Consulting colleagues

During the period of data collection and analysis both authors were working at the Twynstra Group. Hans Bakker was at that time the managing partner of the Business Community practice area, in which Jeroen Helmink also worked as a management consultant.

We want to thank our colleagues, who contributed in many ways to our attempt to unravel the complexities of business integration.

Hans J.C. Bakker
Jeroen W.A. Helmink

1

CASES IN INTEGRATION MANAGEMENT

❖

INTRODUCTION

Research has shown that most integration cases do not provide the benefits that were expected. Peter Drucker (1992) considers that 40 per cent are 'a complete failure', and that only 20 per cent are successful. Reseach by Palepu (1996) showed that, on average, only 33 per cent of the premium that is paid is recovered by integration. Reed Lajoux (1997) presents (among other data) the examples of post-merger failure research shown in Table 1.1.

A story by Sirower (1997) accurately portrays the dilemma that most companies face.

Table 1.1 Examples of post-merger failure research.

Study	Year	Companies	Percentage failed	Primary reason for failure
Brjoksten	1965	5409 acq.	16%	Poor technology assessment
McKinsey	1979	116 acq.	77%	Poor post-acquisition integration (slow pace), overestimation of synergies, large target size, overbidding
Healy *et al.*	1992	50	40% in year 5	Low combined asset productivity
Mitchell/EIU	1988–1996	150	70%	Poor planning, poor communication, slow integration

> Imagine you're running in a treadmill. You can average a speed of 5 km/h, but next year you'll have to run at 6 km/h and in two years 7 km/h. Synergy means that you will have to run even faster, while the competition is giving you a headwind. When you pay a premium for that synergy, the right to run harder, you will have to carry a heavy backpack. And the longer you postpone the forecast increase in speed, the steeper your path will be.

So, managing integration is not an easy task. The high failure percentage proves that. Despite these warning signs, mergers and acquisitions have become a part of everyday life in today's business world. The organizations that engage in them have valid reasons for incorporating them into their business strategy.

This chapter presents cases in which the targeted integration benefits were not realized. The reasons why vary from lack of strategic basis, ill-managed realization and no integration plan available, to ignoring the importance of integrational learning. They show that ordinary large companies have trouble with integration management. The only thing is, you have to do something about it.

We start with three cases which all looked very promising initially but failed anyway, as the media later accurately described. On pp. 5–10 we present a more in-depth picture of a business integration project. We have written this story based on a number of real-life cases to illustrate some of the major dilemmas in an integration project.

PROMISING CASES THAT FAILED

THE CASE OF KNP BT

KNP BT was formed in a three-party merger in 1992, involving Bührmann-Tetterode, Koninklijke Nederlandse Papierfabrieken and the VRG Groep. The merger brought about a conglomerate of three divisions, active in the paper-producing, packaging and distribution (paper, office supplies and graphic industry machinery) industries. The motives for this merger were mostly external and defensive. They involved economies of scale, the need for more control over sales channels, financial synergies, and the desire that the transfer of general management skills should improve performance.

In the five years during which the merged company existed (it was split up again in 1998), the original synergy benefits were not realized. In the first three years the company had three CEOs (each of the original companies had had its chance). Three years after the merger, four members of the board left: two because they had reached the statutory retirement age and two because of disagreements on company policy. Needless to say, that was not a good example for the rest of the company.

Paper production and distribution were deliberately not integrated. The sharing of Bührmann-Tetterode's distribution expertise with the paper division of KNP was announced as one of the benefits of the merger, but because interaction to share that expertise was not effectively managed, this was never realized.

The lack of a clear corporate strategy for the newly formed conglomerate was another mistake. Shareholders and the financial press were not convinced of the merger's rationale, and the stock price never rose. The company lacked strategic vision until four years after the merger started. That proved to be too long.

Although the synergies from economies of scale were realized initially, the differences between production and distribution proved to be too great to be complementary. Those differences were in strategic planning horizons, investment needs, and management priorities. In 1998 the paper-producing division was sold off. In return, it received a $900 million stake in the South African firm Sappi and another $900 million in the form of an interest-free loan. Shortly after, the company had to write off $300 million of the equity stake in Sappi. Analysts reacted negatively to this sale. The conglomerate received less for the paper division than it had invested in new state-of-the-art machinery in the previous year. In the same year, the packaging division was sold to industry competitor Kappa.

The organization's strategy now focuses on distribution and trade after the sale of the paper division. It is now known as Bührmann. The total amount of value destroyed is unknown. One of the former CEOs stated after the split-up that the quality of acquisition strategy will become more important than running day-to-day business.

THE CASE OF AT&T AND NCR

In his book *The Synergy Trap*, Sirower offers the following case as illustrative of a lack of strategic basis.

AT&T bought NCR in 1991, after losing approximately $2 billion in its own computer division. It paid a premium of $4.2 billion, which was 125 per cent above market value. Charles Exley, then president and CEO of NCR, accused AT&T of 'trying to rescue their failed strategy for marketing computers'. After paying such a huge premium, AT&T let the top management of NCR continue as if nothing had happened. They were even given charge of AT&T's old computer production and marketing division. The only thing that AT&T wanted was for them to 'search for synergy'. Their vision was that computers and communication would converge, but the technological advantage of AT&T was in telecommunication switches, not in computers for consumers or business.

When revenue decreased in 1993, AT&T showed up with a strategy for NCR – a bit late. It appointed Jerre Stead as head of the computer division, but this didn't bring synergy either. Between 1993 and 1995, most top managers left NCR. Costs rose dramatically when hundreds of new sales teams in different countries were set up and the company was forced to enter new markets and industries where it didn't have any experience.

The result of all this was that AT&T's shareholders lost the total premium that was paid to the shareholders of NCR. In 1995, these losses added up to $720 million.

THE CASE OF A MERGER IN THE DUTCH UTILITY SECTOR

In 1998, four major power production companies had almost finished negotiations in a prelude to a merger which had started many years before. The producers (EPON, EZH, UNA and EPZ) and their sector organization (SEP) wanted to merge into one new mega-company called GPB. This new large company would then be able to compete in the liberalized European energy market.

The Dutch minister of Economic Affairs approved the merger. The strategic rationale was clearly defensive, as in a liberalized European energy market the new concern would still be relatively small, but it would be less vulnerable to foreign takeovers. In the Dutch market, the GPB would have to give up some market share because of anti-trust regulations, but this could be made up for by better opportunities in the European market. Their costs would have been among the lowest in western Europe and GPB had excellent expertise in the building and exploitation of various power plants.

The process of deal making was very complex. This was partly due to the number of stakeholders involved and the complexity of their different interests. These involved regional government institutions and energy distribution companies as shareholders, the power production companies themselves, the experts that made the financial calculations, the future CEO of the merged company and the ministry of Economic Affairs. This last party played a special role, because at the same time legislation was changed that set out the conditions for the merger and the role of the new power company. The government had to implement the consequences of the European policy of liberalization that opened up the domestic market. At the same time it had to protect the medium-sized and small energy consumers so that they would not have to deal with the negative consequences of free competition.

The negotiations ended because the shareholders of the new GPB couldn't agree on the business strategy for the company. The distribution companies (as buyers) wanted a low-cost, efficient company that would charge low rates. They also wanted to negotiate fixed energy prices for the next 10 years. Others argued that, in a liberalized market, the energy price should be set by market conditions. The government shareholders wanted a business strategy that would generate maximum profits. In the end, the parties could not come to an agreement and the negotiations were called off.

Some involved later said that it was a shame that the deal didn't come through, because it would have been an ideal merger, with positive sides for all. The parties in the energy market, power companies as well as distribution companies, now have to find other ways to strengthen and prepare themselves in order to survive in a liberalized European energy market.

Looking back, the political nature of the strategic decision-making process played a major role and prevented a positive outcome.

FROM 'SUCCESSFUL' ACQUISITION TO INTEGRATION FAILURE: SERVICO AND GERSCO

In order to illustrate a number of traps and issues, we present here the story of two non-existent companies, called Servico and Gersco, which is based on a number of real-life cases.

THE 'OPPORTUNITY' ARISES

Imagine a successful English service company, with a long tradition in the UK in supplying quality services to various English market sectors. Let us call this company 'Servico'.

Over time the founders of Servico have made way for new management and the company has grown. In the last decade growth has been above 10 per cent per annum.

In the last couple of years, many debates have taken place among the Servico Board with regard to the future. New clients that have been acquired have more and more of an international orientation. The service markets that Servico operates in have also become more European in certain sectors. What should Servico do? Should it maintain its strength in its UK customer base and focus on their needs or become a European company?

In the meantime, Servico participates in several loose networks in Europe to meet some of the most pressing needs of its clients regarding an international approach. Partly through these connections, a Board member learns at a network dinner that a German owner/president is thinking about selling his business. He is in his late fifties and has recently expanded his business in Germany, but due to his family situation he wants to retire early.

Our Servico Board member meets the German owner, and from the start the chemistry is there. They like each other and mutual respect grows. Fairly quickly the German owner, who has heard favourable stories about Servico (which is five times the size of his company - let us call this company Gersco), starts discussing his situation with the Servico Board member, who sees a golden opportunity to fulfil his wish to make Servico a more international company.

GRASPING THE OPPORTUNITY

After a couple of weeks the two men meet again and start seriously discussing the opportunity. Gersco, which has offices in three locations – the original one in Berlin and those more recently acquired in Frankfurt and in Hamburg – seems to link well with Servico. Initially both men make quite rapid progress until the Board of Servico has to be brought in. Visits between both Boards take place. After a lot of deliberation the Servico Board hesitantly decides to agree to a due diligence investigation because several competitors seem interested in a deal with Gersco as well.

NEGOTIATIONS

Negotiations start and go quite well until a number of issues arise – among others, there are difficult pension issues for the senior staff. Ambiguities in underlying labour contracts delay the negotiating process, which after several months seems almost to have slowed to a halt.

In the meantime, the Servico Board has informed its employees about the planned acquisition. A significant part of the management and staff recognize the need to move forward. Suddenly, the risk of a failed acquisition seems quite real because of the high cost and risks that seem to have become part of the deal. Serious doubts arise again about the need to go international and about the deal at hand. Negotiations stop and then start again.

The president of Gersco is a decent man who really wants to sell. He likes his English buyers, so he is willing to renegotiate some parts of the deal as long as he can get out of the company in the next six months.

THE DEAL

Finally, after many months, assisted by several financial and legal advisers, a deal is made which is enthusiastically announced by Servico and Gersco. A cash transaction with the German president/owner of Gersco takes place and he is allowed to leave the company within six months. The director of the Berlin office will become general manager of Gersco in Germany and will be the link with the Board of Servico. No other changes are made at Gersco.

STARTING THE INTEGRATION: GETTING TO KNOW EACH OTHER

Several of Servico's British managers design an integration plan and budget to ensure that the integration will work. Unfortunately, the Servico Board decides against this plan. They consider the cost too high and assume that normal working relations will ensure significant synergy.

A large number of people travel to Berlin and other locations to discuss many topics. The financial managers visit their German colleagues. Of course,

IT people from Germany come over to the UK to look at the systems that Servico has in place. Sales staff also meet in various locations to discuss potential clients and look for possible joint clients. Marketing staff in both countries learn about each other's methods.

Because of all this travelling, it seems sensible for facilities management staff to get in touch and see what should be done in this respect. They cannot agree on a facilities management policy (due to local differences) and it is decided to set this issue aside and revisit it later. Thus travel continues and so do the related costs. As a temporary measure, staff are asked to travel as much as possible by car to save money.

ISSUES SLOWLY BECOME MORE OBVIOUS

A serious struggle between 'Berlin' and the other two businesses has been going on for the last year and a half. Since 'Frankfurt' has been bought, the Gersco general manager and that of the Frankfurt office have been fighting for control and to become the most favoured second-in-command to the president.

Without knowing this, the Servico Board has agreed to appoint the Berlin manager as the general manager for Gersco, and by doing so they have estranged the Frankfurt business in a serious way. In the old situation, the Gersco president, due to his ownership and stature, held the company together. But Servico has agreed to his departure within six months of signing the deal.

Soon after he leaves, the first signs of struggle become obvious. Frankfurt so far has asked for direct reporting to the Servico Board because of the different markets they are in as well as the different ICT systems they are using. Initially, this issue is ignored, but the Frankfurt management becomes more adamant.

Gersco's management starts to ask for more input and data from Servico. Of course, that is promised by the Servico Board, who interpret this as a sign of cooperation. In practice, a few serious problems arise once it becomes clear that most of the material (including the company magazine) from Servico is in English, and a number of German colleagues have difficulty reading this.

The Servico Board is therefore careful not to put too much pressure on the Germans to deliver the performance information since they themselves cannot deliver the promised business and company information in German.

WORKING TOGETHER: A DISCOVERY

Some time after the deal is signed, a client with locations in both Germany and the UK approaches Gersco for an integrated deal. This is the ideal opportunity to work together, so managers from both companies sit down together to develop a proposal to meet this request.

The senior sales manager from Germany, who knows this particular client quite well, organizes the proposal and the British give him their input. He makes the final offer and negotiates the final deal on his own with the client, who he knows well and assumes would be surprised if a British manager were to come along. The deal comes through, so a celebration is in order. The first shared assignment has been achieved.

However, after some time a problem arises with delivery in a British branch of the client. It is nothing serious and can easily be repaired, but it needs an understanding of the contract in order to be resolved in an effective way. Only then does it become obvious that the German and British ways of working are not as similar as was assumed earlier when the contract was made.

SIGNS OF SERIOUS PROBLEMS

This and other issues lead to a number of rumours that the German management is actively discouraging its staff from cooperating with the Servico staff in cross-border deals. These rumours come through the ranks and are reported to the Servico Board, which does not want to recognize them.

They have to face another issue: the Board member who made the deal with Gersco accepts an offer to become Chairman of the Board at another company.

After the Servico Board regains its balance, it has to make a decision about who should manage the Gersco company in Germany, and in what way. They appoint another Board member to be responsible for the Gersco subsidiary. Of course, this new Board member needs time to familiarize herself with the situation as well as needing time to get to know the German managers. The German general manager uses this situation to strengthen his position opposite the Servico Board and his Frankfurt colleague.

During this period, sales continue to go down in Hamburg and the Frankfurt operation is incurring rather high costs. The German general manager is slow in pointing these developments out to the Servico Board. Once the Board finds out, he tries to explain these developments by pointing out that some large customers of the Hamburg office have merged and have chosen other service suppliers. The cost increase is seen by him as a temporary issue. At the same time, he underlines the need for Servico to invest in Gersco to demonstrate its commitment.

THE END

Gersco's financial results are not satisfactory. After a while, the newly responsible member of the Servico Board gets really worried. Therefore she decides to send more troops from Servico's headquarters to Germany. Gersco's systems are now rapidly replaced with Servico's systems so that financial and operational data are directly available to Servico's management. Once these systems have become operational, the performance problems become clear to their full extent.

The Servico Board now understands how big the issue is and that drastic measures are needed to solve these business problems structurally.

At this point, several of Servico's competitors again demonstrate their interest in the German operation, i.e. in Gersco. The Servico Board is approached with a very attractive offer, particularly when the current performance of Gersco is taken into account. They decide within a week to sell Gersco to one of their competitors. This will result in a loss because the price that is now being offered to Servico is a lot lower than the price it paid two years ago. But when the possible additional losses are taken into account should the Gersco adventure be continued along the current lines, this seems like a good way out. So they use this opportunity, sell Gersco and start breathing normally again.

WHAT WENT WRONG WITH SERVICO AND GERSCO?

It will be clear by now that the answer is not an easy one. You might even be tempted to ask what did not go wrong? As is common with case studies, many elements have been put into one situation to make it easier to understand once you analyse the case carefully. Remember: this was done deliberately and with hindsight.

Being part of an integration adventure is not something scientific. As our case shows, personal factors as well as 'accidents' play an important role. Look at the start: despite long debate among Servico's Board, it is difficult to discover a clear strategy. Opportunity knocks, personal chemistry helps – and we are under way! Unbelievable? Read the chapter about strategic decision making – especially the section about current practices. If you think this is not for you, read the statistics presented in the first section of this chapter!

Making an M&A deal is work for specialists, but not only for them. Managers should use their business knowledge and not leave their common sense at home once they start with such a process. With hindsight, anyone will agree that when the founder/president/owner leaves a company, especially soon after a merger, this cannot be done without significant consequences which need to be remedied. This is even more the case if the president is still responsible for a significant part of the sales and the account management and image of the company. The president's role inside the company and influence on company culture cannot be overestimated.

Of course, the lack of a clear integration plan and budget is fatal for results-driven business integration. Here, the Board of Servico thought, like most other Boards – see Chapter 3 – that they had already spent enough money. So now it was business as usual. Yet, as the case description shows, a great deal of costs are incurred due to acquisition, but in an unplanned and uncontrolled way. Issues are dealt with one by one with no clear strategic or operational framework, leading to a lot of sub-optimal results. Why, one wonders, does travel to subsidiaries in warmer countries increase in winter time? Or to attractive ski resorts in the right season?

Furthermore, the influence of culture and language cannot be overestimated. We will come back to these in the chapter on management of the soft side of business integration. This case shows only some of the more basic issues which need to be addressed if one wants to avoid being surprised by these phenomena too often, and which almost always have a detrimental impact on performance.

Linked to these issues are those of management style. How do you want to manage your company? Can you translate that directly to the acquired company? The case illustrates the point that this needs reflection and clear and consistent behaviour aligned with the corporate strategy.

And of course, there are still other factors. For now, we hope to have demonstrated the complexity of the issue.

CONCLUSION

Many factors played a role in the cases described in this chapter. In the last case, it was the process of strategic decision making itself that was the problem, while in the case of AT&T and NCR it was the bad strategic rationale that led to failure. In the case of KNP BT it was, among other things, the poor integration strategy that finally killed the merger.

These are but a few cases to demonstrate how difficult it is to perform a merger or acquisition, let alone integrate one. You can probably think of a few further examples yourself. We want to contribute to better integration by providing you with practical experience from the companies in the research and our frameworks. You will find them in the subsequent chapters.

2

THE BUSINESS INTEGRATION APPROACH

❖

INTRODUCTION

As was shown in Chapter 1, business integration projects are usually very complex. They also have a low success rate. These are both reasons for serious concern.

Based on our experience, we have developed a framework which aims to help top managers to become more successful in dealing with the complexities and uncertainties of business integration. This framework we call the Business Integration Approach.

In this chapter we present an outline of this approach. It is the basis for the remaining chapters of this book.

THE BUSINESS INTEGRATION APPROACH: AN OVERVIEW

Business integration is the term we use to describe all ventures or projects that are initiated by top management with the objective of changing the current enterprise by either acquiring or merging with another company or combining two or more previously separate entities inside the existing company.

Our Business Integration Approach (BIA) is an integrated framework designed to deal with the realization of business integration, whether by a merger, an acquisition or internal integration. It consists of several elements which are linked together. Each of these elements will be described in the following sections of this chapter. These are:

- Key design factors
- Programme management
- Integrational learning
- Six phases

No single element will guarantee success, but when used as a consistent framework the BIA allows managers to have more control over the change processes mentioned before.

FOUR PHASES IN IMPLEMENTATION

When we started working on business integration projects, our role as consultants was focused on helping clients with projects that had encountered such serious problems that they could not solve them themselves.

These problems were always implementation-related. A deal had been made, the integration process had started and unexpectedly problems had arisen in one or more areas. Often these were people-related, but they could also be operating model-related. Alternatively, the project had become too difficult to control and was losing momentum: costs were increasing quite rapidly without the expected quick return on the benefit side.

Our efforts were therefore focused on the realization or implementation stage of business integration. The original model that we designed to structure the implementation efforts (Bakker *et al.*, 1998) is presented in Figure 2.1. This

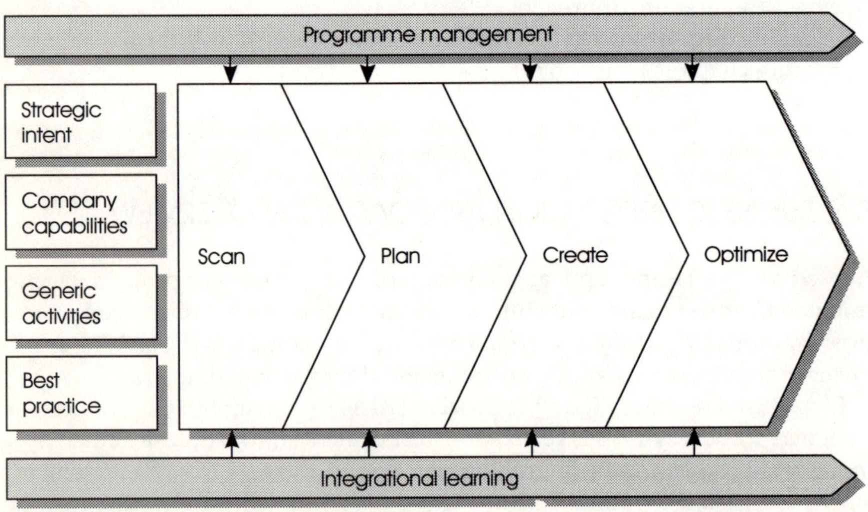

Figure 2.1 The Business Integration Approach.

clearly reflects the design factors, programme management and integrational learning mentioned before.

SCOPE OF BUSINESS INTEGRATION

But where does business integration actually start? You will get a different answer depending on who you ask. Many top managers are tempted to say that business integration starts with implementation, meaning that strategic decision making and deal making have nothing to do with it. A number of corporate finance consultants would confirm this because they see the pre-deal activities as their territory and as a financial and legal issue.

In practice this has led to a situation in which several processes take place almost independently of each other. One is the definition of a business strategy. Separately, whether driven by that strategy or not, a deal is made in which a company is acquired. Only then will the integration be planned and started. The Servico and Gersco case is a nice example of this sequential or disconnected approach (see also Figure 2.2). Situations like this are often driven by opportunities which are simply grabbed. What remains then is the management of the integration. As it turns out, this is the hard part.

This sequential model has clear advantages: quick handling of the deal by a small team results in a deal which, once it becomes reality, will be translated into a business integration project.

As has been shown, in reality this approach also has some serious shortcomings, such as unfeasible integration programmes, irrational synergy estimates and the absence of a commitment to realization. All the participants in our study recognized the need to improve the quality of decision making in the deal phase by taking the integration perspective into account.

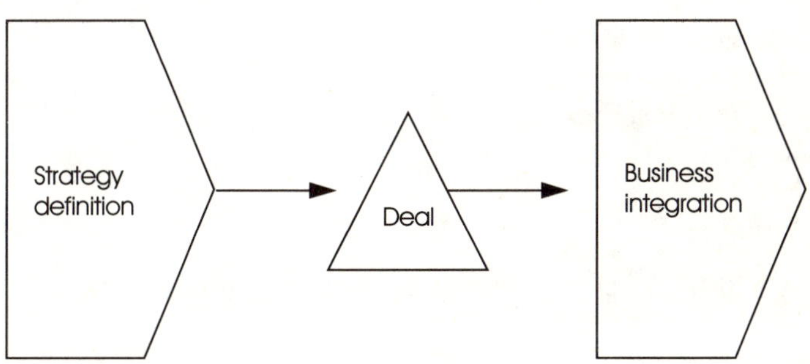

Figure 2.2 The sequential model.

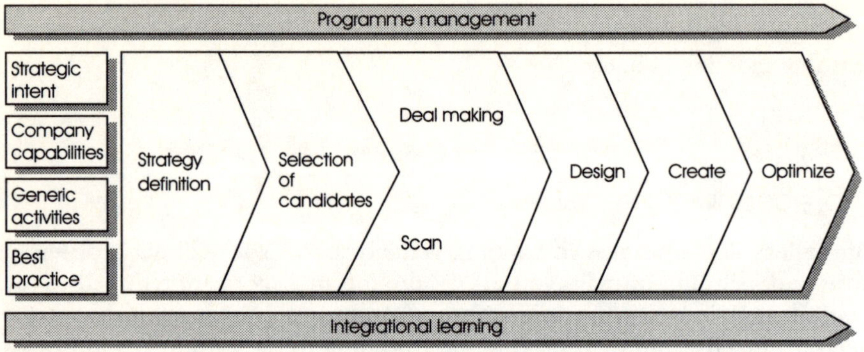

Figure 2.3 The upgraded Business Integration Approach.

THE UPGRADED BUSINESS INTEGRATION APPROACH

The realization that business integration starts when strategic decision making begins is also supported by the experience of GE Capital, who realized after years of experience that integration is not just a stage following the deal. They feel that that kind of approach is less than effective, and causes slow and costly integration. They state as lesson 1:

> Acquisition integration is not a discrete phase of a deal and does not begin when the documents are signed. Rather, it is a process that begins with due diligence and runs through the ongoing management of the new enterprise.

These experiences have led us to fine-tune our Business Integration Approach, as shown in Figure 2.3.

This framework combines our earlier business integration approach with the strategy definition, selection of candidates and deal making.

Our upgraded Business Integration Approach now encompasses the following six phases:

- Strategy definition
- Selection of candidates
- Scan and deal making
- Design
- Create
- Optimize

Each phase will be described briefly in the following sections.

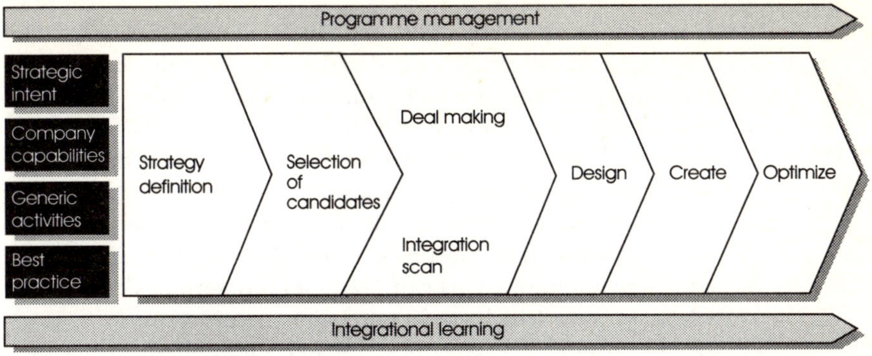

Figure 2.4 Key design factors.

KEY DESIGN FACTORS

There are four factors (highlighted in Figure 2.4) that shape the starting point and internal environment of any integration venture:

- *Strategic intent*: The strategic rationale for a merger, acquisition or internal integration will primarily determine all integration management decisions and activities. Therefore it is critical to understand the strategic drivers for integration.
- *Company capabilities*: The frequency of acquisitions, joint ventures and strategic alliances will determine whether a company has built up effective processes and skills for managing the integration of companies. For example, General Electric's GE Capital division has built up a database of best practices over a period of more than three decades. The essential integration management skills and lessons learned are captured and passed on through the company. However, the frequency of deals done by GE Capital is not typical. Most companies do not integrate very often, and for this reason a company must assess its own capabilities in integration management.
- *Generic activities*: Although each integration effort is unique, there are many activities that will always need to be done. This set of activities generally includes:
  - Ensuring customer retention: customers need to be informed about the integration as soon as possible.
  - Managing investor relations: proactive communication should be set up to ensure that the appropriate information is received by the investment analysts and leading financial media at the right time.

- ❑ Managing employees: it is important to recognize that the employees must break with the past and that the integration involves psychological adjustments. This process must be managed in order to ensure that employees continue to be motivated and carry out their work effectively and also to gain their commitment to the actual integration work.
- ❑ Manage regulatory 'bodies' carefully. Works Councils, unions and governmental approval commissions should receive adequate attention. This can pre-empt any serious delay in the whole process which could endanger the momentum.

❍ *Best practices*: Beside the activities already mentioned, which are generic to each integration, best practices should be used to increase the success rate of the integration and to broaden the scope of the efficiencies to be captured. Their availability will depend on whether or not the company has put energy into collecting, implementing and using the best practices in business integration.

The factors mentioned above will shape the starting point for a company that is planning a merger or acquisition.

INTEGRATION PROGRAMME MANAGEMENT

In any business integration venture, multiple objectives must be realized with regard to many aspects, such as product portfolio, business processes, information systems, culture (value and beliefs), and the organizational structure. Many activities and projects will be needed to realize these objectives.

In our Business Integration Approach, the concept, tools and techniques of programme management (Figure 2.5) are used to manage the integration. Programme management is seen as the answer – based on long-term experience – for planning and controlling such complex ventures as business integration. In Chapter 4 we will not only present an overview of current and best practices in this area, but will explain this part of our Business Integration Approach more deeply and link this framework with best practices, as defined by a group of experienced managers.

INTEGRATIONAL LEARNING

The key success factors in business integration are focused on people-related issues. In the majority of cases these so-called 'soft side' issues are the main

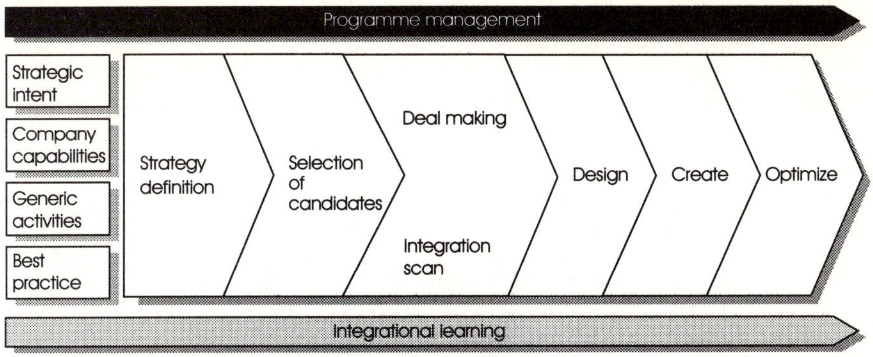

Figure 2.5 Integration programme management.

cause of failure. Getting to grips with these issues has been an important method of improving the success rate of business integration.

In the Business Integration Approach, a dedicated and unique technique for the management of soft issues has been developed (Figure 2.6). It is called integrational learning because it is focused on learning how to integrate and use this knowledge to bring business integration projects to a successful conclusion.

Integrational learning is seen as the key to managing the soft side of business integration because it links organizational development with personal development in a strategic framework and a change process context. It is, of course, part of the overall integration programme management, but because of its crucial role we have decided to discuss this element in detail in Chapter 5.

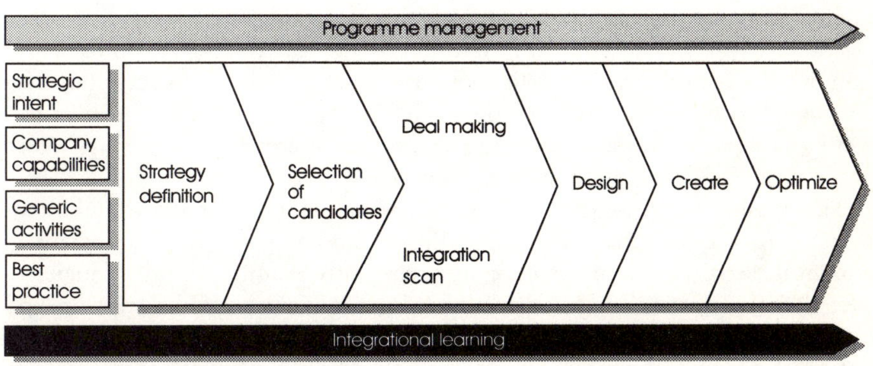

Figure 2.6 Integrational learning.

BUSINESS INTEGRATION PHASES

The various phases of business integration are highlighted in Figure 2.7.

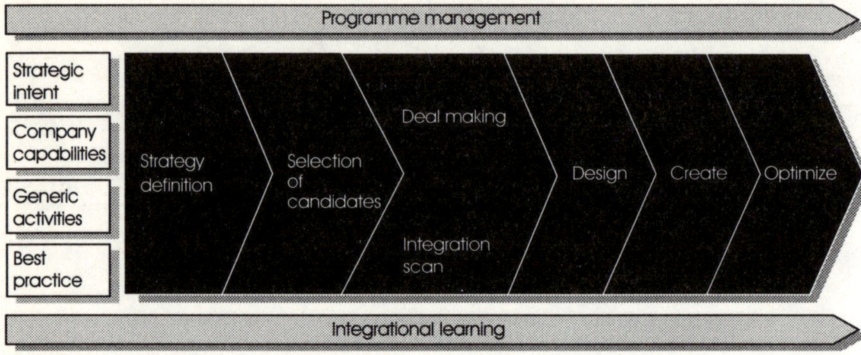

Figure 2.7 Business integration phases.

PHASE 1: STRATEGY DEFINITION

The key question that has to be answered here is: how does business integration management play a role in defining the growth strategy for a company?

Business strategy

As we have seen earlier, mergers or acquisitions are often the result of an opportunity that arose suddenly. Although the business world today is high paced, and agility may be essential to survive, in the long run it is necessary to establish a view about both the industry's and the company's future.

For example, Hamel and Prahalad have clearly stated the need for competitive thinking beyond today's industry structure. That means that companies need to develop a clear view about how they are going to develop or grow in relation to their own industry in order to be ready for the industry of tomorrow. This thinking enables them to ensure continuity in their business and helps to make the company less sensitive to industry dynamics. In this way, a company can start building critical competences by learning from acquisitions and mergers that bring new markets or technologies.

The mission and long-term vision will determine whether and what kind of mergers or acquisitions will bring value to the company. It is important to communicate the desired direction and make sure that the actions of management are supportive of this direction. Communication of the mission and long-term vision is needed to guide corporate actions and helps employees to define their own contributions to the company's future. Business strategy should be explicit, something that can give direction and meaning.

Business Integration therefore starts with revisiting the defined business strategy because this provides the framework necessary for guiding all other activities. If the strategy is not available or unclear, it should be defined before the next step can be made.

Merger and acquisition strategy

The second step in this phase concerns the need to develop a clear merger and acquisition strategy derived from the (long-term) business strategy. When looking for business opportunities that match the M&A strategy, a more balanced and satisfactory decision can be made. A plan can also be developed to achieve the necessary business integration to build on the competences needed to compete today and in the future.

From the business integration perspective an M&A strategy should contain at least three elements. First, it should be clear what kind of growth will have to be achieved via mergers and acquisitions in the years to come. Second, the kind of deals should be defined: mergers or acquisitions? With what kind of partners? Third, it should make clear the level of integration that is needed.

In Chapter 3 we will discuss the issues related to the required business integration benefits in more detail.

PHASE 2: SELECTION OF CANDIDATES

Once a merger and acquisition strategy has been developed, candidates can be sought and screened. In order to do this effectively, one needs to know what to look for: it is essential to have criteria to hand.

These criteria serve as a vehicle for discussion about the purpose of mergers, acquisitions or internal integration. Understanding the criteria thoroughly increases the quality of the process, since all parties involved know exactly what benefits are sought and why these benefits have to be achieved. Also, having criteria to hand increases the chance of finding a candidate that really brings value and offers realistic chances of success, rather than simply grasping opportunities that come by.

Marks and Mirvis (1998) present two sets of criteria that might be used. The first is a generic set of criteria that guides a company's integration programme and strategy. These are characteristics of organizations that must be present in any candidate:

- The right management skills must be available.
- The reasons for sale must be appropriate.
- The market and customer approach must be comparable.
- The organization must be healthy.

The second is a set of criteria that must fit a specific partner. These can be:

- financial criteria
- market portfolio structure
- geographic distribution
- industry position
- brand image
- quality of care
- values and beliefs

In this phase attention should be given to defining and using a broad set of criteria. Having decided on the integration benefits aimed for as well as on the level of integration, business integration-related criteria should be taken into account in selecting possible candidates. This selection process may be realized in various ways. Ultimately, a long list of candidates will be reduced to a short list of acceptable candidates which will be taken into the next phase.

PHASE 3: SCAN AND DEAL MAKING

In this third phase we recognize two steps, which should be carried out in parallel in order to result in a good deal. Deal making is the step that is focused on the financial and legal (or contractual) part of business integration, whereas the scan step focuses on the scanning of all other relevant aspects.

Integration scan

The integration scan is primarily focused on determining the validity of the strategic objectives, assessing the feasibility of the objectives, setting up the necessary generic activities to start the integration, and the alignment of the major stakeholders. It also deals with the programme management issues and the process of integrational learning.

Part of the scan is a broad fit analysis which helps to recognize both the differences and similarities in many areas of the business strategy and business model between the companies involved.

Not only is it important to define the objectives so that they are clear, measurable and understandable, it is also important to check whether the conditions for integration are 'right', using a fit analysis.

Deal making

Based on the outcomes of the earlier phases as well as of the integration scan, deal making comes to an end in the negotiations that are needed to finalize the deal. How a deal is made can vary from case to case. Usually, with mergers and acquisitions, there will be the signing of a letter of intent, a due diligence investigation based on a briefing document, and the actual negotiations leading to the deal (or not).

The essence of our upgraded Business Integration Approach here is that the so-called traditional deal-making activities are extended to include the results of a broad integration scan.

In Chapter 3 we will look more closely at various aspects that determine the success of a business integration project at this stage. At that point we will address a number of process issues that seriously affect the outcome of this phase. Finally, we will provide a framework for handling the various activities in this phase (Chapter 3, Part III).

So far, we have talked about mergers and acquisitions. In Chapter 3 we will look into the special case of internal integration, since there are some differences that should be taken into account, apart from the overall similarities.

PHASE 4: DESIGN

The Design phase contains the activities which will deliver the design of the business model of the integrated entity, the building of capabilities and the engagement of a larger group in the actual integration, as well as the implementation plan, which will guide the venture through phases 5 and 6.

This phase can result in a revised business strategy, a new vision, or a different product and market portfolio. Depending on the type of integration, one or more elements of the operating model will be involved.

The operating model of a company is the description of how a company operates and gives content to its:

- business processes
- organizational structure
- culture
- management systems
- infrastructure
- information technology

Figure 2.8 presents the scope of this phase: the integration of the two business models into a new one. This new operating model describes how the new entity will work in practice.

PHASE 5: CREATE

The actual start of the realization of integration is the next step in our six-phase business integration approach.

The objectives are to achieve the pre-set goals of the basic level of integration. Due to their profound impact, business integration objectives can hardly be achieved in one go. Realizing a merger is not done in one simple step. This

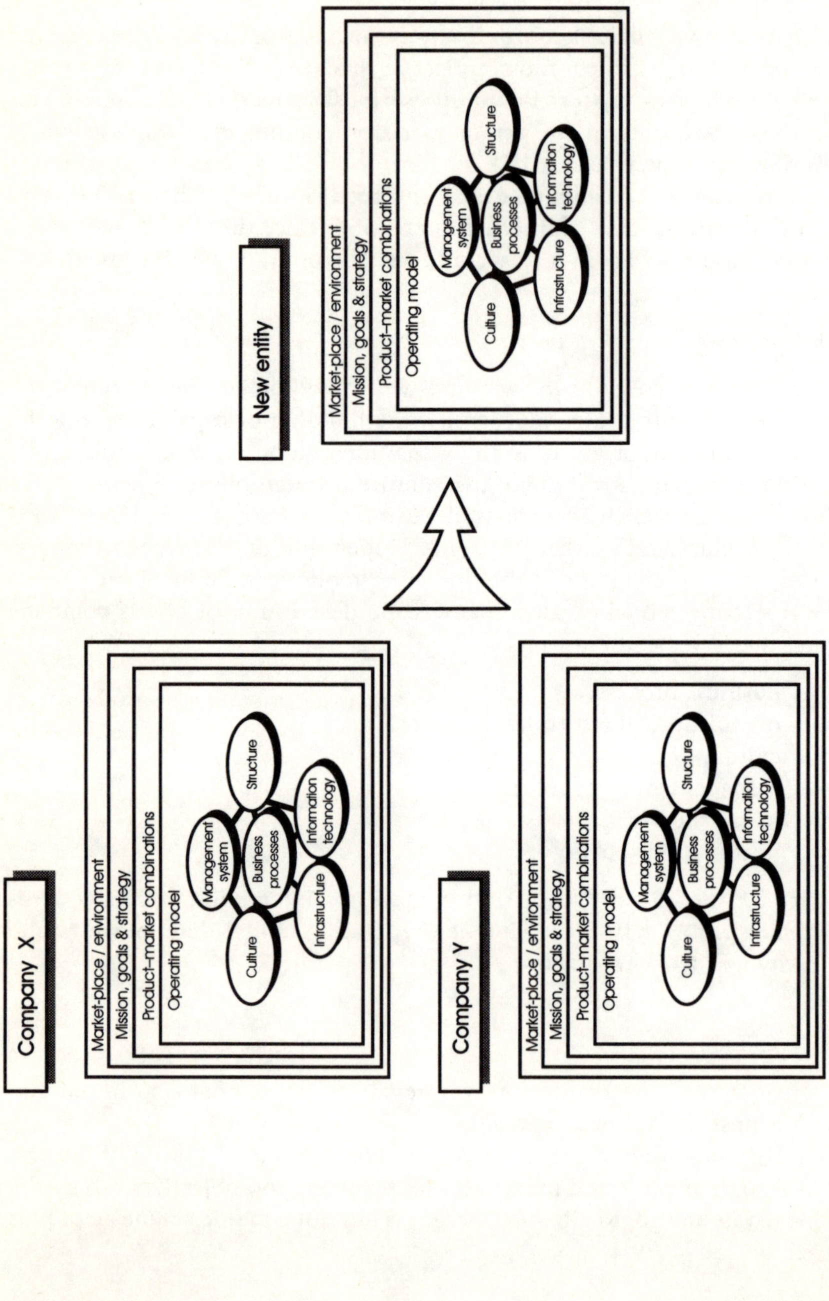

Figure 2.8 Business model integration.

phase ensures that the change process really gets off the ground by realizing some basic changes so that the integration becomes irreversible.

The hard work done at phase 4 of the project should begin to deliver results at this stage.

Because of the uniqueness of every business integration, it is very difficult to present an adequate picture of the precise activities in this phase. Suffice it to say that they will affect all aspects of the operating model and their consequences will be visible and involve all shareholders.

PHASE 6: OPTIMIZE

The last phase in the integration will be focused on finalizing the project. Building on the basic integration achieved, the efforts are now focused on realizing the full benefits of this business integration. This can take a lot of time, sometimes up to several years.

It is an important phase because the integration process will have been under way for some time, and management might be tempted to focus on new ventures and lose interest in this one.

If not enough attention is given to this last phase, the full benefits of the integration will never be realized. There is even a danger of destroying a lot of already-achieved integration (and value) from phase 5 because of the failure to recognize the importance of this phase and not performing the right activities.

At the end of this phase, the integration programme will be closed down. Line management will take over all remaining activities. To increase the competence of the company in integration management, an evaluation should be done that includes collecting lessons learned and best practices. If the results of this evaluation are used well, the company will be able to deal with future projects even more successfully.

CONCLUSION

In this chapter, we have presented an overview of our integrated framework for integration management, called the Business Integration Approach. This will help you to understand the remaining chapters of this book.

In the following chapters, the outcomes of our research will be presented as well as a more detailed look at some of the key elements of our Business Integration Approach.

3

STRATEGIC DECISION MAKING

❖

INTRODUCTION

We start the presentation of our results with this chapter on the strategy and the decision-making process that lead companies to close a deal. Much can be gained, but also lost, in the stages that lead up to the integration venture. If a company buys or merges with another company but pays too much, or does this without having a clear understanding of the benefits it should achieve, it will probably fail, despite excellent integration skills. No matter how good your integration programme is, if there is no synergy to start with (or not enough), you will lose.

The impact of strategic decision making on achieving integration is great. It therefore pays to spend some time and energy on improving the decision-making process.

Overview of this chapter

We start this chapter by presenting the results of our study regarding current practices in Part I. The research focused on integration motives and objectives, company capabilities and the fit between the companies or departments involved.

Part II contains best practices for managing the strategic decision-making process that leads up to closing a deal.

In Part III, a framework for managing this strategic decision-making process is presented. This framework will be based on the best practices identified and adds value with its structure, balance and focus.

PART I: CURRENT PRACTICES IN STRATEGIC DECISION MAKING

❖

We identified two important aspects of the strategic decision-making process. One is the content. What did companies take into account when deciding? What were they trying to achieve? What led them to it? Did they consider whether they would be able to undertake it?

The other aspect was the process itself. How did they decide? Was a deal the result of a quick reaction to a passing opportunity or of long-term strategic planning? Who were involved? What did they learn from it?

INTEGRATION MOTIVES

Why do the companies that participated in the research bother to engage in complex adventures such as mergers, acquisitions or internal integrations? The answer to that question depends upon the type of integration involved.

MERGERS

Mergers were primarily driven by defensive motives, with 'defensive' meaning 'reacting to forces in the market-place that threaten their current market focus'. All mergers that were part of the study were so-called 'horizontal' mergers. Eighty per cent involved former competitors in the same markets and could be classified as 'domain-strengthening' mergers. Only 20 per cent involved domain extension, where existing capabilities were to be applied to new products and markets. This proved to be very hard to achieve successfully.

Almost all of the companies wanted to strengthen their current market position by increasing their size. By doing so they would be more difficult to take over and could benefit from economies of scale. They could also leverage the capital base to increase room for further investments. This was often driven by the internationalization of markets.

The following motives were named as drivers for the mergers:

- increase of investment potential (larger capital base)
- economies of scale (distribution, buying, production, marketing)
- portfolio optimization
- internationalization
- protection against hostile takeovers

- capability transfer in new product development
- capability transfer in marketing and sales

Thus most companies used mergers as a method of consolidation and had a traditional market focus: they looked for partners to lower costs, combine customer bases and leverage current portfolios within their own industry. They did not engage in mergers for value migration, that is to transform the core business of the organization and develop new markets and new capabilities, in order to prepare for future markets.

ACQUISITIONS

Acquisitions seem to be driven by offensive motives, such as portfolio optimization and growth. Some companies considered autonomous or organic growth to be too slow and wanted to gain market share quickly; thus they searched for market share that they could buy from competitors. This could involve their existing market or related markets: approximately two-thirds of the acquisitions in the research were 'domain extensions' and one-third 'domain-strengthening' acquisitions.

The following motives were mentioned as the strategic intent of acquisitions:

- growth
- new market entry
- (product) portfolio optimization
- acquiring a dominant market position
- diversification (value migration)
- transfer of technical/functional skills
- economies of scale in buying
- cost reduction in R&D

The acquisitions were less focused on the traditional market boundaries and operational synergy. Most companies used acquisitions as a way to develop their customer base and expand to new markets, and focused on commercial synergies. Others used it to acquire new capabilities and experience which they could sell in their current markets.

INTERNAL INTEGRATION

In the internal integration cases researched, all efforts were directed towards overhead cost reductions, although there were some benefits to be gained from sharing capabilities. In one case, the company's country organizations in Holland, Belgium and Luxembourg were integrated. There was no longer a need for a business unit for each country. Its market and customers grew

Mergers	Acquisitions	Internal integration
• Economies of scale (buying, distribution, marketing) • Financial benefits (joint investments/new acquisitions) • Defensive arguments (protection against foreign takeovers) • Consolidation of market share in markets that become more international	• Cost reduction in buying, systems integration • Joint product development • Combination benefits from combining market segments • Cost reduction through combination of sales channels • Growth • Value migration	• Cost reduction • Increased need for control

Figure 3.1 Motives for integration.

larger and more internationally oriented. Now the company differentiates only between European and non-European markets. The company needed to increase its control over the business units and try to lower costs, and this was the way to do it. Another internal integration case in our research was done for similar reasons. The market grew and became more 'globalized', with a need for larger segments, more standardized business units and more control. New investments in IT, for example, could be shared, and the need for duplicate systems and infrastructure disappeared. In that way, major cost savings could be realized.

The primary motives are summarized in Figure 3.1.

The companies involved in mergers mostly looked at the evolution of their existing markets and tried to defend their current positions. The maturity of the markets and the market trends associated with this called for economies of scale, a stronger market position and a larger capital base. They could achieve this by merging with their former competitors.

The companies that made acquisitions acted more proactively. They set out ways to develop new businesses and learn new capabilities.

INTEGRATION OBJECTIVES

Although the drivers for integration are generally well understood, 30 per cent of the organizations did not formulate measurable objectives. They knew what it was they wanted to accomplish, but did not bother to quantify it or were unable to. One company explicitly argued the importance of objectives:

integration should be clearly defined in terms of profitability, mission, objectives and shared values. Employees need reasons to understand the importance of integration. Financial targets by themselves do not have much effect on employee motivation.

Another company found it difficult to set objectives and build support for these, because the traditions of objective-setting were very different. They were used to hard financial targets, whereas the acquired company was used to more qualitative objectives.

Most companies only defined the objectives in financial terms.

In general, the companies wanted to achieve one or more of the following: lower costs, share investments, acquire capabilities, market or products, and growth.

In formulating objectives, half of the study's participants took negative consequences into account. These mostly concerned effects on personnel morale and the possibilities of talented individual employees leaving the company and of defecting customers. One company was concerned with the possible reaction of its customers, who would feel that the power of the merged company was too great. It is surprising that although many companies expected some loss of market share, very little was done to prevent this. The research shows that many companies informed their customers by sending them a newsletter and expected them to understand the rationale of the integration. Some companies went further and engaged in proactive interaction with their customers.

Half of the companies did not expect negative consequences, but after the integration programme was over admitted that this was a mistake. One company did not expect the effect of the internal focus on its employees to be that great. It learned that the focus should continue to be on the customer, and that extra attention to service and quality is needed. Another company underestimated the negative reactions and the power of the financial press and analysts. Its stock price fell after the announcement, and it was not able to convince the stock market of the strategic rationale.

INTERNAL CAPABILITIES

As part of the interview, the companies involved in our study were asked whether they had assessed their own managerial capabilities to successfully manage the integration process.

Surprisingly, the integration cases concerned with merger or internal integration did not do this before starting the integration, whereas most of the acquisition cases did. Maybe this is because the benefits that originate from acquisitions are specific and require a special integration strategy that combines the unique competences of the acquirer with the qualities of the acquired company.

With mergers, benefits tended to be rather general and to have more of a cost-cutting nature. This required general management skills, which most companies think they have.

Most of the acquisition cases had prior experience of integration. It is more common for companies to integrate acquisitions than to merge. Acquisitions tend to have less impact on the acquiring firm's identity than mergers do. The size normally differs a great deal, and the acquirer's operating model dominates. This prevents lengthy integration processes where two equal organizations have to decide which headquarters to use, what IT systems, whose procedures etc. More acquisitions can be done in a particular period of time, and they need less energy than mergers.

Mergers have so great an impact on an organization and require so much energy that an organization simply cannot keep up with the same kind of pace that is possible with acquisitions.

FIT ANALYSIS

Another aspect of our study concerned whether or not the fit between the two companies involved would be good enough to be successful.

A fit analysis was formally executed in 30 per cent of the research cases. This meant that these companies formulated important areas that needed to be compatible in order to realize the integration objectives and then assigned a task force to analyse whether the required fit was there or not.

Half of the companies implictly analysed fit, which meant that in the deal-making process both parties talked about their organizations and came to the conclusion that in some areas enough similarities existed to assume that the organizations would fit together. They did not base those conclusions on facts or research.

One fifth of the companies did not address the issue of fit at all.

When considering the compatibility of companies, or 'fit', one can look at many different aspects:

- What do the companies want to achieve?
- What value proposition do they offer their customers?
- How do the two product portfolios match?
- In what markets are they active?
- What is the core competence?
- What are the two cultures?
- What are the terms and conditions in the HR policy?

The areas that were covered in the fit analyses differed between mergers and acquisitions. Mergers generally focused on organizational structure, infrastructure/geographics and product portfolio issues, whereas acquisitions tended to focus on business strategy and product/market portfolios.

In most cases, the cultural fit was said to be medium to low. What is interesting is that 50 per cent thought they knew the cultural differences without analysing them. During the post-deal integration this often caused unpleasant surprises when cultural differences were greater than or different from what was expected.

In the internal integration cases, it wasn't so much the company culture that caused difficulties since both parties belonged to the same company. Instead, because it involved departments in different countries, it was the country culture differences that proved hard to overcome. One company organized training sessions prior to integration to prepare the employees for the differences they could expect and how they could deal with these. In this case, the cultural differences were more easily accepted and dealt with. Employees considered these a 'fact of life', instead of the result of an unwilling attitude from employees in the other country.

The importance of fit analysis depends on the strategic intent and areas of integration benefits looked for. This explains why mergers focus on organizational structure and infrastructure, because their integration benefits usually lie in economies of scale that require full integration. Acquisitions are more market/strategy driven, and therefore focus on business strategy and product/market portfolio analysis.

THE DEAL-MAKING PROCESS

As mentioned in the introduction, there are two aspects of strategic decision making: the content and the process. In the preceding paragraphs the content of the process that the participating companies went through was discussed. Now we consider the process.

PLANNING OR OPPORTUNITY?

Ideally, integration would be the result of a carefully developed strategy. But entrepreneurial spirits would argue that sometimes one has to act on 'gut feeling'. Here is what the companies in our study did.

In 50 per cent of the cases, the merger, acquisition or internal integration was the result of a well-defined business strategy. The companies carefully laid out their strategic path and searched for the possible candidates that would fit in. The other 50 per cent simply reacted to an opportunity, quickly balancing the chances and risks. Our research suggests that it is more likely for acquisitions to occur as the result of opportunities that fit the proactive strategy of growth or development, and that mergers are generally the result of long-term business strategies driven by maturing markets.

The internal integration cases all prepared the decision to integrate very carefully. Two of the three companies started thinking about the integration two years before the actual integration plan was communicated.

PHASES IN THE DECISION PROCESS

One company realized that the way in which it was taking over companies was *ad hoc* and unfocused, and therefore structured the acquisition process. First, it made some strategic choices. What business do we want to be in? What core activities do we want? Do we want to expand, broaden, strengthen or deepen our core activities?

Once it had set out a business strategy, it identified criteria that acquisition candidates would have to meet. This improved the quality of the acquisition process of the company enormously. The buying of small companies, based on doubtful arguments, was no longer considered. There was a clear path laid out.

As was mentioned earlier, 30 per cent of the companies made a fit analysis part of the process, thus bringing in aspects other than strategy alone. They chose a longer and more difficult decision-making process to be sure that what they wanted could actually be achieved.

A case that involved more than one party started when the companies individually came to the conclusion that their industry was changing and they had to develop a vision of their future in this industry. They were already united in an industry platform, and hired a consultant to support the process. By working backwards from their vision of the future, what they needed to do to prepare themselves became clear. Soon, they came to the conclusion that the best way forward was to integrate the different companies and make the best use of each company's specific capabilities and strengths. After setting out the strategy and analysing their compatibility, a plan was laid out to determine how the integration process would have to work.

CONCLUSION

In this part, both the content and the process of the actual strategic decision-making process that the companies went through have been discussed. We have seen that aspects other than strategy and finance alone are important. In the next part of the chapter we will present the best practices that the companies formulated, based on their experiences as described in this part.

PART II: BEST PRACTICES IN STRATEGIC DECISION MAKING

❖

INTRODUCTION

As part of our research, the managers were asked to define best practices for the process that leads up to the closing of the deal. These best practices contribute to making the right choice for the right integration partner. They build upon lessons learned the hard way and advice from industry leaders.

The best practices are ranked in order of importance by the managers involved and a brief description is given for each.

BEST PRACTICES IN STRATEGIC DECISION MAKING

1. ANALYSE AND EVALUATE THE STRATEGIC VALUE

Although this seems a rather general remark, taking a step back during the decision-making process to analyse and evaluate the strategic value of the planned integration venture is crucial for success. The question you should be asking is: how does this contribute to the realization of our overall business objectives? A formal point in the process to evaluate the results so far will help to prevent a hasty, badly informed decision.

2. ACT ACCORDING TO AN EXPLICIT (ACQUISITION) STRATEGY

When there is no explicit (acquisition) strategy present, integration cannot be part of the planned realization of the company's business objectives. Opportunities will arise and possible candidates will need to be reviewed. An explicit acquisition strategy serves to assess whether or not an integration opportunity is aligned with the corporate strategy and will provide strategic benefits. Without this, discussion will be based on subjective arguments. A clear acquisition strategy will reduce uncertainty, guesswork and discussion and will ensure a well-balanced strategic decision about whether or not to integrate.

3. UNDERTAKE DUE DILIGENCE ON ALL RELEVANT ASPECTS

Very often, due diligence is only performed on financial and legal aspects. This can result in an integration rationale in which only certain benefits are mentioned. What is forgotten is that there may be some aspects present in the candidate's situation which prevent the benefits from being realized. If, for example, a brewery is acquired in country A, with the integration benefits lying in the combined distribution of local brands and foreign brands, but country A has import restrictions on foreign beer, the integration benefits will never be realized. Although this may seem an obvious point, it is important not to overlook it.

Therefore it is important to undertake due diligence on all aspects:

- business strategy
- product and client portfolio
- operating model
- legal, financial and tax issues

4. MAKE SURE THE RIGHT MANAGEMENT SKILLS ARE AVAILABLE

Managing an integration process requires very different skills from day-to-day operations management. Integration management requires:

- programme management skills in order to keep the integration on track and deliver the result in time
- communication skills to successfully communicate the vision, integration rationale, integration results and so on in order to rally support and keep up company morale
- political skills to handle unproductive politics that arise, and sensitivity to balance hard and soft dilemmas.

An assessment of management skills can prove whether these skills are available; if not, it must be ensured that they will be by the time the integration starts.

5. ENSURE TOP MANAGEMENT ALIGNMENT AND COMMITMENT

Commitment to the targeted integration benefits from top management prior to closing the deal is vital. Without this formal and public commitment, there is no guarantee of the energy and support that will be needed in the realization phases and no guarantee of the feasibility of obtaining the benefits. Many studies have been done on the role of top management in mergers and acquisitions. Some theorists say that the ego is one of the primary drivers for mergers and acquisitions. It is also a major factor in integration failure. Without the alignment and commitment of top management, priorities will be unclear, political manoeuvres will undermine authority, the necessary capacity (time, money, resources) will not be allocated and so on. Without it, there is no basis for success.

6. ANALYSE THE FIT

Differences in company culture have caused many integration efforts to fail. We have also seen that not all organizations analyse these differences before making a deal. Without analysis there is no chance of making a proper assessment of the role that cultural differences will play in integration success, nor in the managerial response to it. Cultural fit is not the only important aspect that needs to be analysed though. Strategic, market portfolio, value discipline, operational and geographical fit can also be important. The focus of fit analysis will depend on the kind of benefits that are perceived. By using a good fit analysis, something can be said about the compatibility of a potential integration partner and the probability of integration benefits being realized.

7. DEVELOP ACQUISITION STRATEGY FROM BUSINESS STRATEGY

A good acquisition strategy should make clear why acquisitions are essential in realizing the business strategy. The rationale for acquisition should originate from sound business strategy arguments.

8. PERFORM A STRATEGIC RISK ANALYSIS

Sometimes, engaging in a merger or acquisition can have adverse effects on corporate image. Moreover, competition is likely to react in a way that challenges the drivers for integration. In the snack sector of the retail market in the USA, one company that produces snacks engaged in an alliance with the largest retailer to optimize in-store performance. The competition answered with new product launches, discounts and package style changes because they knew that the internal focus would seriously affect the snack producer's agility. With that move they were able to capture extra market share in an otherwise difficult market. The company in this example did not analyse what the reactions of their competitors would be. In the food industry in particular, marketing tactics can have a dramatic influence on performance, and competition is very hard. This reaction could have been predicted if the company had thought about strategic risks in the decision-making process. It could then have taken precautionary measures. A strategic risk analysis forces you to think about the risks involved and what kind of action you would take if these were to occur. It enables you to react more effectively to events which could ruin the success of your integration.

9. STIMULATE INTERACTION BETWEEN THE CORPORATE M&A TEAM AND THE TEAM UNDERTAKING THE ACTUAL INTEGRATION

Interaction between the two teams broadens the scope of the strategic decision-making phase. Through interaction, a better informed and balanced assessment of the candidate for integration can be made.

10. DECIDE ON THE APPROPRIATE INTEGRATION FORMAT

It is very important to have an understanding of the way you want to integrate after the deal is closed. Not only can this be a point in the deal-making meetings, it also gives an insight into the feasibility of the intended benefits and shapes the implementation design.

11. DEFINE CLEAR AND SIMPLE ACQUISITION CRITERIA

Clear and simple acquisition criteria help to make a well-founded decision about whether or not to integrate and prevent a company from being surprised by an opportunity, being hasty in its decision making and ending up with a bad decision. The criteria can be developed from the acquisition strategy.

12. DON'T OVERESTIMATE POSSIBLE SYNERGIES: BE REALISTIC

One of the biggest mistakes made in mergers and acquisitions is the overestimation of possible synergies. It happens all too often that managers are surprised when synergies turn out to be much lower then expected. Realistic synergy forecasts increase the likelihood of success, ensure moderated decision making and prevent unpleasant surprises such as unachievable goals in the realization phase.

13. DETERMINE HOW READY THE ACQUIRER IS FOR AN ACQUISITION

An acquisition, merger or internal integration can never work if your own organization is preoccupied with great organizational changes, does not have the right attitude or skills available, or other factors are not right. It demands great concentration, a positive attitude and specific skills in order to be successful. A discussion about this can reveal potentially valuable information which should be taken into account when shaping the implementation plan.

14. CHECK THE FEASIBILITY WITH THE INTEGRATION TEAM

A one-sided evaluation of the integration effort can mislead the decision makers and present those responsible for the implementation with an impossible task. To prevent the integration rationale from being too one-sided, careful consideration must be given to the way in which the benefits will be realized. The integration team can check whether the planned synergies are realistic and feasible. Otherwise, no fair judgement can be made, and synergy fairytales can cloud managerial decision making.

15. ANALYSE WHY A COMPANY IS FOR SALE

Sometimes company shareholders can have a specific interest in selling. Buying a company in need (the 'knight in shining armour' scenario) demands a very hands-on, decisive approach if success is to be achieved. The risks involved should be carefully considered.

16. ANALYSE EXISTING MANAGEMENT CAPABILITIES

Managing interaction and integration requires specific skills, different from normal management skills. An assessment of skills can lead to a different allocation of management or development programmes to provide the necessary basis for success.

17. BE VERY SELECTIVE WITH CANDIDATES FOR INTEGRATION

Not every candidate matches, although there probably is no one best solution. Do not be easily impressed; stick to the appropriate steps in decision making.

18. DECIDE WHO IS RESPONSIBLE FOR INTEGRATION

Unclear responsibilities may lead to surprises. Clear responsibilities right at the start give the individuals involved a chance to prepare themselves and provide input to the process. Let them give their commitment to the promised result publicly.

19. DEFINE MEASURABLE, CLEAR AND REALISTIC SYNERGY BENEFITS

Synergy benefits that are not defined in clear, realistic and measurable ways will never be met, and you will never be able to say whether the integration was a success or not. Measurable benefits enable progress control and managerial intervention. Clear, realistic and measurable benefits can also be used in programme control, progress communication, evaluation, remuneration and employee motivation.

20. SET MEASURABLE INTEGRATION PROCESS TARGETS

Integration process targets enable the integration manager to assess whether or not the integration is on track, whether action is needed and whether the end targets will be met, and allow progress evaluation with stakeholders.

21. MAKE AND USE A SCRIPT FOR THE STRATEGIC DECISION-MAKING PROCESS

There has to be a clear understanding of the steps that must be followed in the decision-making process to prevent a hasty, unbalanced decision. Evaluation of previous decision-making processes may improve the quality of decisions that are made.

22. WATCH OUT FOR INTEGRATION WITH TOTALLY DIFFERENT CULTURES

Imagine that you are a life insurance sales representative in a large American insurance company that decides to engage in a mega-merger with a large American bank corporation. Top management sees great synergy benefits in cross-selling each other's products via the combined sales channels. Suddenly you have to work together with a former potential competitor. And it was hard enough working together with the guys from travel insurance!

Now imagine that the bank corporation isn't American, but German. Imagine the language problems and the differences in management style, risk-taking attitude and so on. This adds a whole new dimension to an already difficult challenge. It takes great effort to understand another culture and successfully work together to realize the integration benefits.

23. ASSIGN CLEAR TASKS AND ALLOCATE RESPONSIBILITIES

An integration process is the ideal situation for unrest, politics and endless debates to grow. Eventually this will cause the failure of any change project. Assigning clear tasks and responsibilities helps to prevent failure. This means not only assigning clear responsibility to the integration manager, but also making clear who will take decisions, who will participate in the preparations, who will take care of corporate communications to stakeholders and so on.

24. MAKE AN OUTLINE OF THE INTEGRATION PLAN AS PART OF THE FEASIBILITY STUDY

Part of understanding the feasibility of certain integration benefits depends on insight into the way the integration will take place. Only when operational managers, together with the M&A team, have developed an outline of the integration plan, can it be evaluated whether, under the integration plan conditions, integration is still favourable.

25. CHECK WHETHER THE MARKET AND CUSTOMER APPROACHES ARE COMPATIBLE

Imagine a company totally dedicated to delivering superior service to its customers merging with a company that values hassle-free, low-priced standard products. The mind-set, values and beliefs that lie at the heart of the employees of both companies will differ greatly, along with management systems, service policies, quality control and so on. Integrating these very different companies will involve making a choice in favour of one 'value discipline'. It will take a lot of energy and time to incorporate the two into one way of thinking, let alone the effort that will have to go into communicating this to customers.

26. TAKE YOUR TIME (DON'T LET THE HEAT OF THE MOMENT GET TO YOU)

A difficult process such as this should never be hasty, even when the opportunity is good and time is limited. It can lead to unbalanced and hasty decision making.

27. TAKE NEGATIVE RESULTS INTO ACCOUNT

Very few companies mention the possibility of negative results in their press releases. This should always be taken into consideration. An evaluation of this scenario can bring up helpful ways to prevent negative results and may even lead to planning adjustments.

28. ASSESS THE CONSEQUENCES OF FAILURE

Figure 3.2 (Sirower, 1997) shows the effects of delaying the realization of integration benefits. If a company A acquires another company B, which is worth £25 million, on average it pays a 40 per cent premium of £10 million. This means that the company has to generate extra performance, on top of the individual performance expectations of both companies. So if company A acquires company B, it will not only have to realize its own profits and those of company B, but also extra profits to pay back the premium. In the figure, the required extra performance improvements that need to be realized from year *i* onwards, over a planning horizon of 10 years, are shown*. Note that these are just to break even: if these extra benefits are realized the premium is

					Year i					
£ Premium	1	2	3	4	5	6	7	8	9	10
£10 M	£1.99 M	£2.41 M	£2.95 M	£3.66 M	£4.62 M	£6.00 M	£8.10 M	£11.65 M	£18.82 M	£40.46 M

Figure 3.2 Required performance improvements.

* $$RPI = \frac{\text{£ premium}}{\sum_{t=i}^{N}\left(\frac{1}{(1+r)^t}\right)}$$

r = cost of capital (15 per cent); RPI = Required Performance Improvements; N = planning horizon; i = year in which benefits start

merely covered. It demonstrates that if you are not able to realize the integration benefits in the first two years, the required performance improvement each year from year 3 onwards is increased by 50 per cent.

29. NO QUICK AND DIRTY DECISION MAKING

If the opportunity does not permit a proper decision-making process, the chances of surprises in later stages increase to unacceptable levels. Don't let all the excitement of the process get to you. Although this is easier said than done, a conscientious approach may provide the necessary time to look things over.

30. ALIGN AVAILABLE COMPETENCES WITH REVISED STRATEGIC GOALS

Sometimes a merger, acquisition or internal integration involves a shift in strategic direction. For a different strategic direction, different competences may be needed. This is often forgotten, and the old allocation of employees and competences is retained. In this way, the new strategy will be very hard to put into practice. (Imagine a manager whose competences lie in delivering superior lead cycle times and low costs with standardized products, but who now has to be able to deliver full service with a semi-customized product line.)

31. IF THE POST-ACQUISITION PROCESS ISN'T CLEAR, DON'T DO IT, EVEN IF THERE IS A STRATEGIC FIT

If the post-acquisition process isn't clear, the feasibility of achieving the targeted benefits cannot be assessed. Nobody should agree to close the deal without really being sure that the benefits can indeed be realized.

The chance of unexpected barriers or negative consequences is too high to risk the normally substantial premiums.

32. THINK ABOUT THE TIMING

Which moment provides the best opportunity within your own organization and what is the best time in the market to start the integration? Answering these questions and incorporating them into your planning may increase the quality of the integration process, since the environment will be at its most favourable.

33. HIRE AN OBJECTIVE VIEW/INPUT

Most strategic decision-making processes are accompanied by investment bankers. They will be in favour of closing the deal, because their fee depends on it. If you want to make sure that you are getting professional, objective arguments, hire an outside consultant to bring in experience, expertise and objectivity. Experienced acquirers achieve better post-merger returns because they are more likely than inexperienced companies to have the right vision and to implement it effectively and quickly. If an inexperienced acquirer wants to achieve these things, it may hire one or more outside parties who can help it form, implement and accelerate a post-merger strategy.

34. DOUBLE THE COST BUDGET AND TIME TO INTEGRATE AND THEN SEE WHETHER THE MERGER OR ACQUISITION STILL MAKES SENSE

It is not uncommon for a complex change project to cost more than twice the original budget and take twice as long as expected. When this is taken into account, it may lead to a very different outcome of the decision-making process than was made by the initial optimistic planning and budgeting.

35. DECIDE ON THE INTEGRATION SPEED PRIOR TO CLOSING THE DEAL AND TAKE THE EFFECTS INTO ACCOUNT

There is a dilemma in integration speed. Most people say that integration must be done quickly and decisively. But this doesn't allow for detailed planning, research and the involvement of large numbers of employees. It is good to consciously deal with this dilemma (involvement vs. speed) and make the effects explicitly clear in communication of the planning.

36. MAKE THE DECISION ON INTEGRATION STRATEGY BASED ON SCENARIO ANALYSIS

Scenario analysis can prove a good instrument for discussing several integration strategies because it forces a group to think about possible outcomes and the different ways of dealing with problems. In doing so, it increases the quality of planning, broadens the scope and deepens the content.

37. CONSIDER ALTERNATIVE CHOICES AND WEIGH THEM AGAINST THE OPPORTUNITY AT HAND

It can be hard to assess the value of an opportunity when you have no comparison. Comparing the opportunity with others gives explicit guidelines for discussion and displays the consequences of the final decision.

38. ONLY INTEGRATE WITH HEALTHY ORGANIZATIONS

Organizations that are preoccupied with internal or external problems do not have the right capacity, attitude and energy to deal with the complex consequences of integration. Since the basis of integration will be weak, it may be better not to start at all.

39. MAKE A BOARD MEMBER RESPONSIBLE FOR THE ACQUISITION AND LEARNING STRATEGIES

As we said earlier, experienced integrators have a better integration scorecard than inexperienced ones. In order not to let slip the valuable lessons learned in previous integration efforts, it is a good idea to make someone responsible for the active learning from integrations to improve the skills for next time. This individual may be the same person as is responsible for the acquisition strategy that provides the basis for the strategic decision-making process.

Table 3.1 shows the average scores for the aforementioned best practices.

Table 3.1 Best practice average scores.

	Generic practice	Average score
	High to very high contribution	
1	Analyse and evaluate the strategic value	4.6
2	Act according to an explicit (acquisition) strategy	4.5
3	Undertake due diligence on all relevant aspects	4.5
4	Make sure the right management skills are available	4.5
5	Ensure top management alignment and commitment	4.4
6	Analyse the fit	4.3
7	Develop acquisition strategy from business strategy	4.3
8	Perform a strategic risk analysis	4.2
9	Stimulate interaction between the corporate M&A team and the team undertaking the actual integration	4.1
10	Decide on the appropriate integration format	4.1
11	Define clear and simple acquisition criteria	4.0
12	Don't overestimate possible synergies: be realistic	4.0
13	Determine how ready the acquirer is for an acquisition	4.0
14	Check the feasibility with integration team	4.0
15	Analyse why a company is for sale	4.0
16	Analyse existing management capabilities	4.0
17	Be very selective with candidates for integration	4.0
18	Decide who is responsible for integration	4.0
	Medium to high contribution	
19	Define measurable, clear and realistic synergy benefits	3.9
20	Set measurable integration process targets	3.8
21	Make and use a script for the strategic decision-making process	3.8
22	Watch out for integration with totally different cultures	3.8
23	Assign clear tasks and allocate responsibilities	3.8

Table 3.1 *(continued)*

24	Make an outline of the integration plan as part of the feasibility study	3.8
25	Check whether the market and customer approaches are compatible	3.8
26	Take your time (don't let the heat of the moment get to you)	3.8
27	Take negative results into account	3.8
28	Assess the consequences of failure	3.8
29	No quick and dirty decision making	3.8
30	Align available competences with revised strategic goals	3.6
31	If the post-acquisition process isn't clear, don't do it, even if there is a strategic fit	3.6
32	Think about the timing	3.6
33	Hire an objective view/input	3.5
34	Double the cost budget and time to integrate and then see whether the merger or acquisition still makes sense	3.5
35	Decide on the integration speed prior to closing the deal and take the effects into account	3.5
36	Make the decision on integration strategy based on scenario analysis	3.4
37	Consider alternative choices and weigh them against the opportunity at hand	3.4
38	Only integrate with healthy organizations	3.3
39	Make a board member responsible for the acquisition and learning strategies	3.2

Scale: 1 = Very little contribution to success, 5 = Very high contribution to success

PART III: FRAMEWORK FOR STRATEGIC DECISION MAKING

INTRODUCTION

So far, we have looked at what the interviewed managers did to make the right decision in a number of business integration projects. Then we presented what, according to them, are best practices in strategic decision making.

In this final part of the chapter we will present strategies for improving the strategic decision-making process of the Business Integration Approach (Figure 3.3) in which the defined best practices are taken into account.

As we described earlier, we feel that it is important to take integration issues into account during the first phases of strategic decision making. All too often decisions are made in these phases that prove counter-productive in later integration phases. We feel that by providing strategies for improving strategic decision making the actual integration process itself could become easier. The motivation for this framework has been presented in Parts I and II of this chapter and in the cases examined in Chapter 1.

One of the most important things is to define the benefits that you want to realize in a realistic and measurable way. This should give an idea of the ideal level of integration and therefore give direction to discussions about what to do and what not to do. We also think that the selection of candidates and deal making should be influenced by the later integration challenges. Finding a candidate that matches your integration criteria and signing a deal in a controlled manner will improve the quality of later integration outcomes. In this last part of Chapter 3 we will put forward some strategies to realize this.

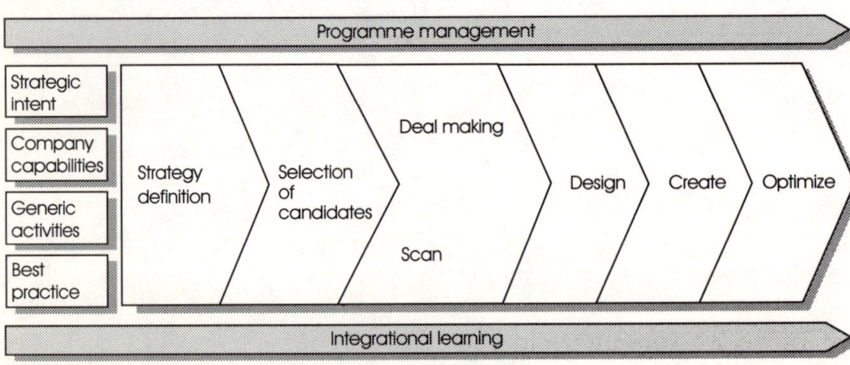

Figure 3.3 The Business Integration Approach.

The six sections in this part cover, respectively:

- identifying the integration benefits
- the level of integration
- improving the deal-making phase once a potential partner has been selected and deal negotiations have started
- the special case of internal integration
- the key roles in the M&A decision-making process
- the process issues of decision making

IDENTIFYING THE INTEGRATION BENEFITS

In the Business Integration Approach, a strategic intent matrix (Figure 3.4) has been developed that can be used to define the objectives or benefits for a merger, acquisition or internal integration.

The kind of benefits to be realized greatly influence the kind of integration effort. Therefore we will discuss some basic patterns of strategic intent to make clear what kind of integration consequences follow from this M&A phase. More insight into this matter allows the deal-maker to take business integration aspects into account when determining the M&A strategy and closing the deal.

We will discuss the following topics:

- sources of benefits
- scope of benefits
- examples of using the model
- patterns in benefits

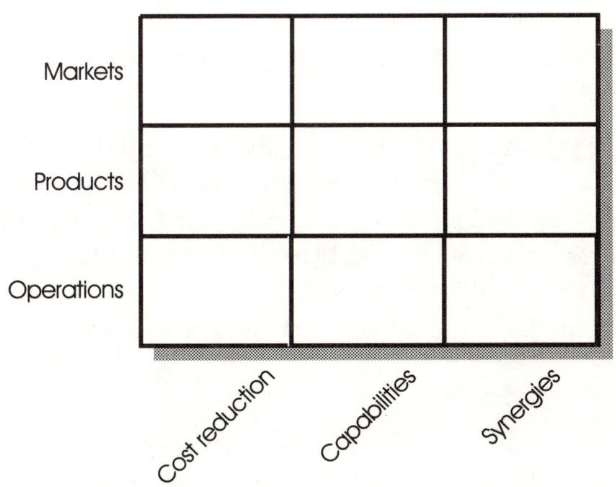

Figure 3.4 Strategic Intent Matrix.

SOURCES OF BENEFITS

The sources of the benefits which should result from a business integration venture are displayed on the horizontal axis. This provides the rationale for strategic decision making. At the same time it focuses business integration efforts in certain directions, in both the pre- and post-deal phases. The amount of benefits will need to be compared with the expected risks, premium, integration costs and strategic implications.

Cost reduction

Cost reduction is focused on lowering costs per unit by combining activities. The efficiency theory views integration as a rational choice to achieve advantages, which can be divided into different sorts. Operational synergy can be divided into economies of scale and economies of scope.

Economies of scale will reduce average costs as a result of the more efficient use of combined resources. This kind of efficiency will occur in the integration of similar organizations with similar products in the same or related markets, because the scale of production or distribution of a product or service only grows when they are supplementary, rather than complementary. Economies of scope will enable the company to deliver a greater amount of products or services from the same inputs compared with what it could deliver before integration. This kind of efficiency will be achieved when different but related products or services are produced or handled together.

Ansoff (1968) identified (among others) the following cost reduction synergies:

- *sales synergy* (when the distribution channels, sales administration, staff, marketing and logistics can be combined to work for an integrated product portfolio)
- *operating synergy* (more efficient use of the means of production and people, a greater basis for overhead allocation, joint purchasing contracts etc.)

Financial synergy occurs when the cost of capital of the acquiring or combined firms will be lower. The capital base will be larger, which enables the financing of more and larger investments. Financial diversification is also an advantage. This occurs when the other firm has a different industry cycle. Integrated cash flows will be more stable and the variations in performance smaller. Other financial benefits include tax advantages and insurance gains.

Capability transfer

Capability transfer is focused on the (mutual) exchange and application of capabilities. We use the term *capabilities* as a synonym for competence, expertise or knowledge.

Examples include the acquisition of an ill-managed firm and replacing the existing management with the acquirer's management team, or an acquisition to buy specific capabilities, such as foreign market introduction, advanced production techniques, or R&D knowledge and skills.

These kinds of benefit will need careful integration management because capabilities are generally hard to transfer. A distinction must be made between capabilities that rely on explicit knowledge, which can be transferred in physical form (such as plant layouts, R&D formulae and patents), and tacit knowledge, which is gathered through experience and learning. These can be transferred by socializing (doing things together) (Boekhoff *et al.*, 1998). Capabilities are generally built through a lengthy process of trial and error. For the most part this is also the reason why companies acquire or merge: because they neither have nor take the time to build those capabilities themselves.

Synergy

Synergy is the most frequently used word in the arguments that companies use to explain their intentions. But the definition of the word 'synergy' may vary. There can be many forms of synergy.

Synergy can be described as 'the fact that the result of combined handling of different activities in one organization is larger, greater or better than the sum of the results if the activities where undertaken in different, separate organizations'. Sirower (1997) describes it as follows: 'increases in competitiveness and resulting cash flows beyond what the two companies are expected to accomplish independently'. With the same economic input, more output, lower costs or a higher consumer price can be achieved than before.

Synergy, in our view, is the accomplishment of value creation in a way that individual companies seperately cannot achieve. Where economies of scale and of scope can be achieved by internal growth, and an organization can internally develop key capabilities, real synergetic benefits are only achieved when the integrated organizations can transcend industry boundaries, building or developing new products or services that change the industry's future. An example of this kind of synergetic integration is SMART – a joint venture between Mercedes-Benz and Swatch in which capabilities in car manufacturing and development were combined with conceptual design and marketing skills to create a new product concept in the automobile industry: a small car with unique brand characteristics.

SCOPE OF BENEFITS

The vertical axis of Figure 3.4 displays the areas in which the integration benefits are expected. In our model, integration benefits can be found in three areas: operations, products and markets.

Operations

Operations, in our view, involve not only the business processes of a company, such as production, purchasing, logistics and R&D, but also the organizational structure, its ICT, its infrastructure, its management systems, its culture etc.

Examples of this scope can be found in heavy industries, where margins are very low and size in production offers efficiency savings that reduce variable costs and produce more output over which to allocate overheads (and so the capacity utilization can be optimized).

Products

The second area of integration benefits, products, concerns the product (or service) portfolio of a company. An example in this area is an automobile manufacturer that has a product range varying from light city cars to mid-range automobiles. To offer the complete range, the company needs the top class, which it can acquire to complete the product portfolio. The benefits can vary from economies of scope or the transfer of brand management skills to new product development synergies.

Markets

The third area of benefits, markets, refers to the market-places in which the company(ies) involved sell their products. This has to do with reaching the right customers, entering new markets or extending existing markets. An illustration of this scope is a large retail company that has a large market share in its own country. It attracts the right customers, but wants to grow. New markets have to be found, and this is realized via internationalization.

EXAMPLES

Figure 3.5 shows examples of the different focus areas. To illustrate the strategic intent matrix further, Figure 3.6 presents examples for each focus area.

The 'Fortis/Ahold' example for the focus area markets/synergy is not an existing example, but it would fall in that area if the two companies were to integrate: the experience in retailing could help Fortis sell its financial services, while the distribution network and nationwide coverage (Albert Heijn supermarkets) could provide benefits. Other benefits include combined customer loyalty programmes, credit services for household shopping, and client research (setting up client profiles based on shopping behaviour, then customizing financial services based on demographics, risk attitude and so on).

Another example is the intended (but abandoned) merger in the pharmaceutical industry between SmithKline Beecham and Glaxo Wellcome. The pharmaceutical industry is undergoing major changes, involving globalization, concentration and technological developments. The merger would have

	Cost reduction	Capabilities	Synergies
Markets	• Marketing (joined MARCOM budgets) • Cross selling opportunities	• Sharing of market intelligence	• Access to new unrelated markets • Combination of non-related sales channels
Products	• Sharing of R&D investments	• Sharing of R&D expertise • Optimizing product portfolio management	• Combination of unrelated products or brands
Operations	• Economies of scale, scope in production, logistics, etc. • Overhead reduction	• Sharing production or financing expertise	• Revolutionary new production technologies

Figure 3.5 Focus areas.

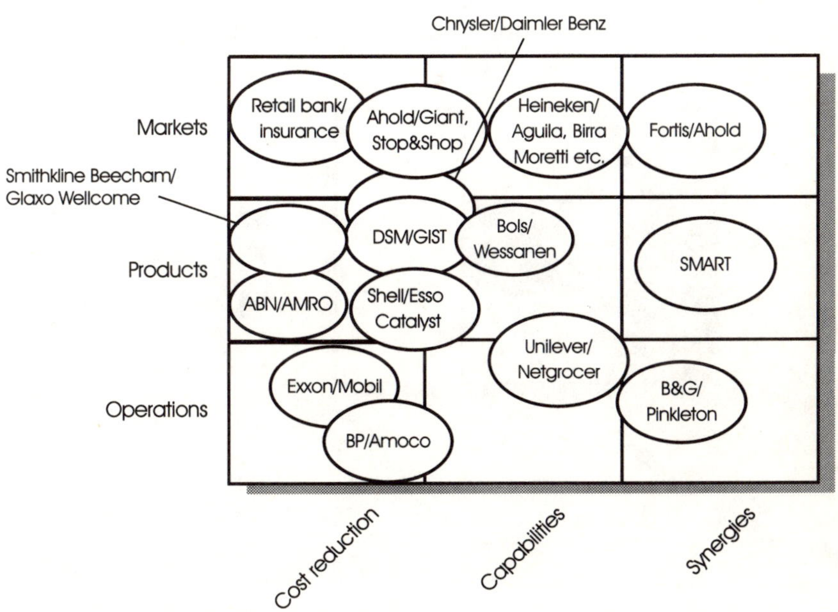

Figure 3.6 Examples of using the Strategic Intent Matrix.

enabled them to share the very large investment requirements in R&D needed to pursue rapid technological developments. They would also have been able to profit from economies of scale in sales, because the sales representatives could make their visits to potential clients (doctors, specialists) with a combined product portfolio, thus offering a broader assortment with the same effort†.

Another example is the Chrysler/Daimler Benz merger, which generated a giant in the automobile industry. Defensive motives, such as cost control through economies of scale and the transfer of internal capabilities (in car production and design, supplier management, marketing etc.), played a major role in the merger, which took place in a rapidly changing industry environment. The benefits lie in cost reduction, capability transfer, operations and products, as well as in markets. The exact priorities between these different areas vary.

PATTERNS OF BENEFITS

Although an integration case will generally be based on more than one focus area of strategic intent, some basic strategic patterns can be identified. The following section presents and explains three basic patterns, and shows what the consequences for the integration strategy are.

The basic pattern of Figure 3.7 focuses on cost reduction. The company involved searches for ways to reduce costs by means of integration. Integration can lead to larger scale, more efficient ways of working and financial synergies through combining the production, staff, finance, or other functions.

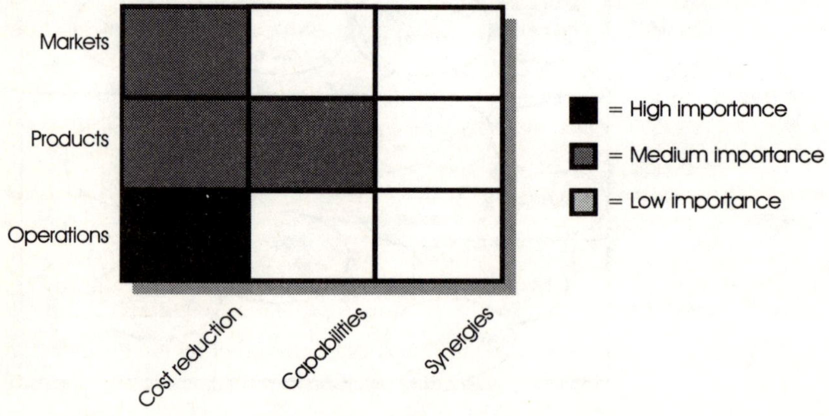

Figure 3.7 Basic pattern A: cost reduction.

† SmithKline Beecham and Glaxo Wellcome subsequently restarted the merger process.

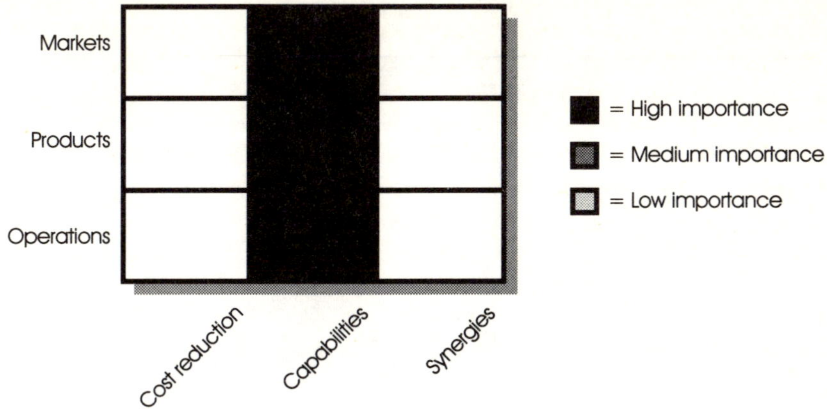

Figure 3.8 Basic pattern B: capability transfer.

If this is to be successful, tight planning and control in the realization phase are needed. Also, clear and measurable targets must be defined and plotted in time. Instruments like Activity-Based Costing, Business Process Redesign, the Balanced Scorecard and the application of IT can be useful in realizing cost reduction. Special attention during the Scan phase is given to the analysis and definition of cost-cutting opportunities. The resistance to change will be great when choices have to be made between the practices of both the organizations involved. Careful planning and handling of these kinds of problems will require great attention. Experts should be used to identify cost-cutting opportunities, introduce and apply tools and techniques, and mediate in best practice definitions.

Companies pursuing the basic pattern of Figure 3.8 want to acquire, combine and mutually apply specific capabilities which will put them in a position where they can compete better. These might be R&D capabilities, technical capabilities, marketing skills or other capabilities critical to the success of the company.

In the Scan phase of this kind of basic pattern it is important to perform a good competence scan and identify which capabilities are the value drivers for the integration. Because the pattern concerns capabilities that are developed through a lengthy process of trial and error and may be tacit (embedded in people), it may be hard to actually transfer the key capabilities. Knowledge management may provide the necessary vision, tools and techniques for successful capability transfer.

For this pattern to be successful, it is important to have a clear understanding of the cultural fit, since the value drivers are so closely connected to people. A cultural fit analysis will need to be performed as part of the due

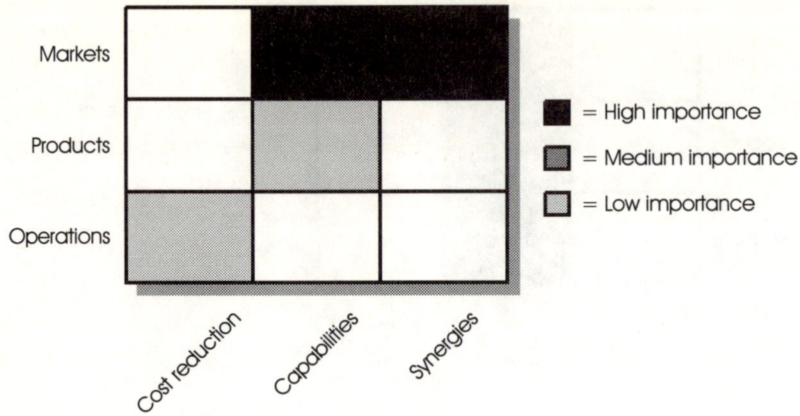

Figure 3.9 Basic pattern C: market focus.

diligence process to determine the feasibility of the benefits. Once the integration has started, it will be important to start to manage the social interaction between the organizational units involved in order to facilitate the sharing and transfer of capabilities. This pattern will generally involve very specific business aspects in which the key capabilities are located.

The market focus basic pattern (Figure 3.9) applies when companies want to gain access to a new market, combine existing markets, and/or combine marketing- and sales-related activities. Instead of profiting from lower costs or specific capabilities, the company wants to optimize its existing market portfolio. This could follow the decline of a company's current market, making it more difficult to achieve the required growth in earnings and profits. An example is a company active in base chemicals that wants to reduce its industry cycle sensitivity. Here value migration to the life sciences sector might be the driving motive.

The benefits of sharing markets and sales-related activities and getting access to new markets are typical of this basic pattern. The focus during integration will be on marketing strategies, product portfolio management, sales and distribution channels. Existing capacity will need to be reallocated, which may affect customer service. It is important to analyse the strategic fit in the strategic decision-making phase. Understanding the other organization's business is essential to develop a successful integration strategy for this basic pattern.

The tactic of acquiring market share and developing technological capabilities can be found in the IT industry, where access to new technology is gained by buying a small company with a specialized product and then incorporating it (Microsoft frequently does this). Another example can be found in the beer industry, where large breweries such as Interbrew and Heineken buy local breweries to acquire a foothold in a specific regional market (Heineken's recent acquisitions in Poland and Spain for example). Here, the motives lie in market expansion rather than completing a product porfolio.

DECIDING ON THE LEVEL OF INTEGRATION

INTRODUCTION

We have seen that there can be different goals for business integration, which all have specific consequences. In order to achieve the integration benefits, the entire company does not have to be involved in every case. Sometimes one need only integrate the financial and legal systems. The level of integration needed depends partly on the strategic intent and partly on the companies involved. The choice of a specific level determines the integration intensity. Therefore, taking the level of integration into account in the strategy definition allows the decision makers to oversee the consequences of their choices and evaluate the options more carefully.

Once the integration benefits that are sought have been defined, it will be necessary to agree the integration strategy that will be used to realize them. The extent to which integration takes place affects the number and nature of integration activities that need to be undertaken, and the organization, time and budget that depend on that.

Although Lajoux (1997) talks about deciding whether 'to integrate or ignore', we assume that integration benefits can only be achieved by some kind of integration, however minimal this may be. By integration we mean creating some kind of relationship between two entities (apart from ownership) that will result in the desired outcomes. This relationship may be limited to a financial level, which implies that (for example, in the case of a market focus pattern; see previous section) the additional market share and turnover can be consolidated. We identified three levels of integration, which will be briefly discussed here.

THREE BASIC LEVELS OF INTEGRATION

Although each integration case is unique, we have identified three basic levels of integration, as shown in the Figure 3.10.

Full integration

This level of integration implies integrating all aspects of the companies or units involved, ranging from the business strategy and PMC portfolio to the operating model.

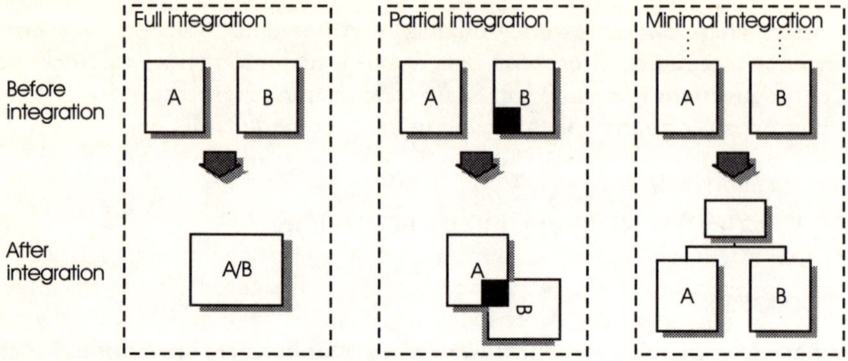

Figure 3.10 Basic levels of integration.

One new company will be the result of this integration process, resulting in a single new business strategy, a shared product and market portfolio, a single operating model and a single financial model. This kind of integration can be accompanied by integration benefits such as economies of scale and cost reduction.

The entities involved will be affected in all key aspects. This kind of integration has many effects on personnel. In some cases, this is the only way to achieve the objectives. Business strategy, staff, business processes in operations, and subsidiaries will all be included in the integration, which results in one new company. The product portfolios will be shared and a single new operating model will result.

Partial integration

This level of integration involves the coming together of some, but not all, aspects of the business; the aspects to be integrated will depend on the specific integration objectives.

Among the reasons for using this level of integration are the balancing of costs and benefits (partial integration generally costs less and it may therefore be essential to accept a lower level of benefits). Also, to avoid unnecessary resistance, it may be decided to involve only part of the organization in the integration process. This is particularly true when cultural differences play an important role in the ultimate success of the integration. Another common reason is the geographic situation: it may be necessary to exclude certain business aspects because the consequences of relocation or transport would be negative. As was the case with full integration, the type of industry will affect the integration level. For example, in the airline industry and travel services sector it is common to integrate back office functions while keeping the front offices separate.

In any case of partial integration, the two integrating companies may continue to have different strategies, but one will always be dominant. The product portfolios can differ, but they may share some products. The operating models may be partially different, but the financial model is shared.

Minimal integration

The third integration level is called minimal integration. In this form, two separate companies or units continue to exist as separate entities, sharing only their financial structures and some corporate procedures. This kind of integration is generally used in financial consolidation and may involve a small amount of transfer of knowledge or key capabilities. New business development strategies generally involve unrelated market acquisitions, where it is essential to give the organizational unit freedom to evolve. Most frequently there is one dominant corporate strategy, various business unit strategies, no joint products and separate target markets. This kind of integration can be found in emerging or fast-growing markets, where it is essential to keep up market share or volume.

OVERVIEW

Table 3.2 summarizes the above-mentioned factors in deciding on the particular level of integration and the definitions of these levels.

DECIDING ON THE LEVEL OF INTEGRATION

It is critical to decide on the level of integration, because this defines the integration activities both before making the deal and in the realization phase. In the pre-deal phase, for example, it will imply looking at business operations for integration opportunities or hindrances, so that a more realistic estimate can be made of the feasibility of integration, the required effort and the related costs. The decision about a particular level of integration will take into account the following factors.

Integration benefits

The decision about the required level of integration is basically dependent on the sources of benefits. In the basic patterns of integration benefits described earlier, it was made clear that cost-cutting benefits will probably involve all aspects of the companies involved, whereas market-focused benefits can also be accomplished by integrating only the customer-focused departments of a company.

When the benefits that a company is looking for all come from one source, they are concentrated. As such, partial integration, limited to that one source, may suffice (e.g. benefits limited to R&D only). If the benefits are spread

Table 3.2 What level of integration is needed?

Aspect	Full integration	Partial integration	Minimal integration
Definition	Integration includes all aspects of the entities involved, ranging from business strategy to operations	Integration includes some elements of the operating model	Integration is limited to a joint financial model and some corporate procedures.
Assumptions	One new company	Two companies or units	Two companies or units
Types of integration benefits	Operations: economies of scale; cost reduction	Specific integration benefits	Financial consolidation, knowledge/capability transfer
Business strategy	Single business strategy for new entity	Separate strategies but one dominant	One dominant corporate strategy and various BU strategies. New business development.
PMC portfolio	Shared PMC portfolio	Differentiated PMC portfolio; possible joint products	No joint PMC portfolio
Operating model	Shared operating model	Different operating models or partially shared operating model	Separate operating models; possibly best-practice expertise transfer
Financial model	Single financial model	Single financial model	Single corporate financial model

though, full integration might be needed (e.g. benefits from production optimization, joint investments and capital base, and transfer of market intelligence).

Industry dynamics and market maturity

When considering integration, industry dynamics can play an important role. In very dynamic markets, the agility of the entities involved becomes an issue.

The maturity of the market that a company works in will also influence its integration benefits and thus the level of integration. In emerging markets, characterized by rapid technological development, growth and many small competitors, a company can pursue a growth strategy by acquisitions. These acquired companies do not have to be fully integrated. In fact, they may need their freedom to react quickly to changes in the market. In maturing markets, characterized by concentration, low margins, fierce competition and low growth, a company will want to reduce cost, in order to improve annual profit growth. Standardization and scale are important, and will require full integration.

Functional dynamics and synergy

Functional dynamics and synergy refer to a focus on cost reduction and the benefits achieved from combining the functional elements of an organization (for example, production or sales). When functional differences are small it is easier to achieve economies of scale. If this is the benefit aimed for, full integration will be required to realize these benefits. In full integration efficiency is likely to be more dominant, while in minimal integration effectiveness plays a more important role.

Type of integration (merger, acquisition or internal integration)

The integration programme in the case of a merger will cover all business aspects. The same is true for internal integration, which mostly concerns the integration of two or more identical departments. Acquisitions, on the other hand, are more likely to differ in size and strategic intent. Not all of the acquiring company's organization will need to be involved in the integration process. For reasons of commercial effectiveness, minimal or partial integration can be considered.

Geography and company/country culture

A local company that merges with another local company will usually have more in common with that company than with a company on the other side of the globe, at least in terms of language, national culture etc. Full integration is more likely, although many other factors play a role here. An acquisition in another part of the world logically generates a geographical or distance issue.

Minimal integration will then be logical, given the practical, cultural and strategical considerations.

Sometimes cultures can differ so much that cooperation is seriously hindered. This can stand in the way of achieving the integration benefits. Minimal or partial integration can help to manage the process of cultural assimilation, provided that the defined integration benefits allow this level of integration.

Integration risks

When the integration is considered to be risky, it might be wise not to go for full integration but to opt for partial or even minimal integration. In that way, if it goes wrong, the damage is limited to a small part of the company.

Company capabilities

If the acquiring company lacks integration capabilities, it may be wise to limit one's ambitions to minimal integration. This, of course, is only a serious alternative if the integration benefits can be achieved with minimal integration.

EXTENDING THE DEAL-MAKING

We are convinced that the quality of the decision making during the deal-making phase depends to a large extent on the attention paid to integration issues.

Using a business integration perspective, we will describe the activities which are part of the deal-making phase (see Figures 3.11 and 3.12).

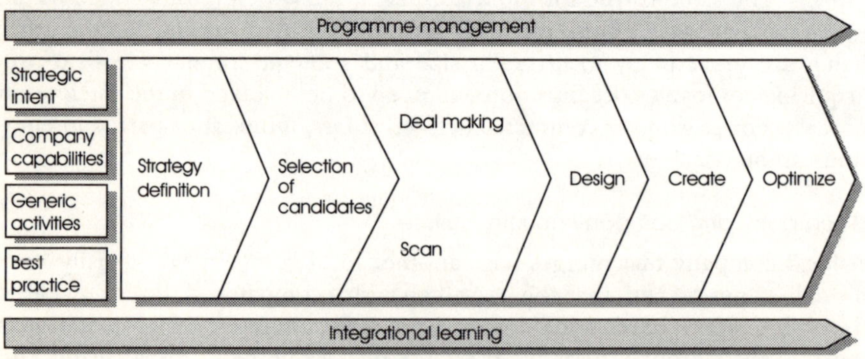

Figure 3.11 The strategic decision-making framework.

Scan
Extended due diligence ❍ Fit analysis ❍ Company capabilities analysis ❍ Timing
Implementation design ❍ Integration targets ❍ Integration strategy ❍ Integration responsibilities ❍ Integration budget
Validate feasibility ❍ Integration risk analysis
Top management alignment ❍ Realization commitment
Integration management contract

Figure 3.12 Business integration issues during deal making.

EXTENDED DUE DILIGENCE

Successful integrators not only know what they are looking for, they also make sure they get it.

Once a candidate has passed all the important criteria, the due diligence phase can begin. Traditionally, this is the field of expertise of the finance department, together with investment bankers and corporate finance consultants. They will analyse the financial, legal and strategic outlook of the candidate. Although this is an essential part of the process, it is not enough to ensure future integration success. A thorough due diligence process must also encompass non-financial aspects and less tangible elements (which incidentally is recognized by most corporate finance consultants nowadays).

What should be addressed in the due diligence process from the integration management perspective?

Fit analysis

A fit analysis must be performed. This will need to focus on strategic, portfolio, value discipline, operational, cultural and geographic fit. In that way, the due diligence team can estimate the potential for success. Some organizations include up to 20 people in their due diligence team. Although this seems a bit crowded and may cause difficult planning dilemmas, it will pay off if something is uncovered that prevents the company from entering an integration which destroys rather than adds value.

A number of capabilities are needed in the team. Financial, legal and tax capabilities are needed to assess the candidate's financial health and the value creation options. The commitment of those responsible for the subsequent integration phase is essential for success. It is therefore important to include them in the due diligence team. Specific capabilities, such as HRM or operations management, may also be needed to look at specific issues.

The involvement of operational management and HRM specialists increases the diversity of the team, fosters discussion about findings and brings about a more balanced and more solidly based due diligence outcome. In this phase, specific objectives can be defined that need to be realized when an integration with a particular candidate is pursued.

Company capabilities

Another aspect of this phase is an honest assessment of the capabilities of both the acquiring company and the integration candidate. A study of large integrations found that 65 per cent of successful acquirers reported managerial talent to be the most important instrument for creating value in a deal (Anslinger and Copeland, 1996). Capabilities must be available to support potential new strategic directions. The managerial skills to run both the operational business and the integration activities must also be available. It is therefore essential to determine whether these skills are available, and the consequences must be taken into account if this is not the case.

Timing

The due diligence team should also make an evaluation of the timing of integration: is their own company ready for such a venture or not? This provides input for both implementation design and planning, as well as the feasibility study in the subsequent phases.

IMPLEMENTATION DESIGN

Based on the outcomes of the due diligence process, the M&A team will decide on the valuation of the company on which the due diligence has been undertaken.

From the integration management perspective the following issues should be addressed in this phase: integration targets, strategy, responsibilities and the budget and time available for integration. These aspects are all seen as part of the implementation design.

Integration targets

The use of specific criteria guided the due diligence phase and resulted in detailed knowledge of the possible sources and scope of benefits. These must be formulated so that it is clear to all the stakeholders involved exactly what benefits should be realized. It is important not to overestimate the benefits.

In the acquisition strategy, the possible level of integration is outlined. In this phase of the process, the chosen level of integration will be detailed, depending on the source and scope of the particular benefits. Identifying which departments will be affected and outlining the new organization allows for more detailed planning and provides information about the size and energy needed to integrate. The design of the future organization makes it possible to oversee the consequences of the integration.

Integration strategy

Now that the outline of the new organization is known, the realization stages can be described to ensure effective control during realization. In order for effective control of realization, process targets (deadlines for intermediate results) should be defined. In that way, progress can be monitored. After brainstorming over the stages and intermediate results, integration speed must be considered. As mentioned earlier, there is a dilemma. Quick and decisive realization often seems to be critical for success, but so do broad employee involvement and commitment. These have to be balanced carefully. After the time necessary to complete all the activities has been estimated, a calculation can be made of whether it is still feasible to realize the integration benefits in time.

Integration responsibilities

The allocation of responsibilities prior to closing the deal enables those responsible to influence the outcome and guarantee realistic preparations. It also prevents unrest from arising when key positions are vacant. There is nothing more disturbing for the decision-making process than people having hidden agendas focused on becoming the new CEO!

Integration budget and time

Internal as well as external aspects may create an unfavourable environment for integration that has an adverse effect on the chances of success (for example, the retirement of a charismatic CEO, labour conditions negotiations, past history of frequent layoffs, new market entries, regulatory changes). Hence the timing of the integration may be important. When the integration strategy is defined, the consequences in terms of budget and time needed for integration should be known. These may act as 'showstoppers'. Integration may be feasible, but it should be possible to do it in a reasonable time and at a reasonable cost. *Reasonable* is a relative term, and follows the equation of premium paid, amount of integration benefits and the time at which the benefits will finally pay off.

If all this is done correctly, it can be used in the communication to stakeholders in the following phases to explain exactly what is going to be realized, when, how, and who is responsible.

VALIDATE FEASIBILITY

The M&A team will analyse the feasibility of a possible deal from various viewpoints, one being the financial point of view.

An evaluation of feasibility should also be done from the integration perspective. All the negative elements must be assessed: do they stand in the way of future success?

One way to do this is to define an integration failure scenario and identify the impact on all aspects of the company (including clients, operating model, finance etc.).

Another way to handle this is to list all the soft-side risks (see also Chapter 5) and decide on possible risk management measures, their impact and cost. If for each soft-side risk the probability of it becoming reality is plotted along with possible counteractions, many potentially destructive events can be identified in advance. This enhances the quality of decision making, because now a decision can be made based not only on what is intended to be realized, but also on unplanned, but possible, scenarios.

TOP MANAGEMENT ALIGNMENT

Before the negotiations enter a critical stage, top management should be on board regarding the planned deal and all its consequences. From the integration perspective, top management alignment is in fact critical in building the necessary support for integration. During this phase, top management has to confront their own views on the integration and discuss them openly.

If the previous phases have been handled according to best practices, many pitfalls will have been avoided. This leaves top management with a sound integration design and plan, clear responsibilities and a fair evaluation of the feasibility of the project. It is now time to rally the necessary support and align all views on future priorities.

The outcome of these talks should be that top management firmly commit themselves to the venture, including the way in which the benefits will be realized, by whom and within what budget – that is, if the necessary support for the project has been given. If there is substantial doubt about the realizability of the intended integration benefits, top management should abort the process at this stage. This may seem a waste of time and money, but if the high failure rate is taken into account this will be a wise decision.

Top management alignment meetings should give the deal-making team a clear remit, with priorities, negotiation margins and targets.

INTEGRATION MANAGEMENT CONTRACT

From the integration management perspective, concluding the deal will imply signing a contract with the managers who have committed themselves to realizing the integration benefits. If the deal made turns out to differ significantly from what has been agreed before, the management contracts drawn up earlier should be reviewed.

INTERNAL INTEGRATION: A SPECIAL CASE OF STRATEGIC DECISION MAKING

Internal integration projects are those where units of a large or multinational company are integrated into a new entity. Recently, as part of regionalization many country organizations have been integrated into regional entities.

Of course, this is not an M&A process. Nevertheless, deciding on an internal integration project is a decision-making process that has – certainly from the integration management perspective – many similarities with an M&A decision process. However, the steps that a company should take to integrate two business units or departments are somewhat different.

The decision about internal integration generally follows these steps:

- explicit business strategy
- clear integration strategy
- implementation design/planning
- validate feasibility
- management alignment
- integration kick-off

You will notice that the partner selection phase is not relevant here.

The business strategy will be translated into an integration strategy that defines what changes need to be made in the internal structure of the company. This integration strategy should define what benefits are needed and which conditions and restrictions apply. Implementation design and planning will be set up within this framework. This can be done as described in previous sections. Also, an investigation into the desired changes in strategy and value discipline should be made, and a new operating model should be designed.

After the new design has been established, an implementation plan will be set up, covering issues like responsibilities, phasing, time planning and budget. Once this has been done, the feasibility of the design should be checked and management should reach a consensus on the design and implementation planning presented. They should give their commitment to it.

When management has agreed to the plans, a kick-off can be organized to start integration. Throughout this process, it is important to pay attention to communication to stakeholders and participation of the works council. A proactive attitude towards these two aspects will generate more understanding and support from employees. This is important for the success of the integration phases.

KEY ROLES IN DECISION MAKING

In our framework, we try to address not only the steps and activities to follow, but also the way in which these activities are performed and by whom – in other words, the process side of decision making. This section outlines several key roles, and the next section will address some process aspects.

The steps in strategic decision making have been described above. There are various stakeholders who have influence on these steps. Some of the stakeholders play an active role. The following roles can be identified:

- CEO
- top management
- M&A team
- integration team

CEO

The CEO has a clear responsibility to define and communicate the vision that underlies an acquisition strategy. This should guide the M&A team in their activities. When the selection of candidates is made, the CEO should review the strategic choices with top executives to build a consensus. During the valuation and deal-making choices, a good relationship with the top management of the other company involved is necessary to build trust and commitment. If necessary, the CEO should participate in the negotiations. When the deal is closed, an important task for the CEO is communication of the intended integration strategy. During the integration phase, the CEO should periodically review progress and provide the necessary resources.

TOP MANAGEMENT

Top management should concentrate on running the business and provide input into the staffing of critical positions. They also have a distinct role in translating the strategic intent and vision into measurable and realistic goals. While realizing the desired level of integration, they should protect the programme from unexpected disturbances and if necessary call for adjustments.

M&A TEAM

The role of the mergers and acquisitions team is to set out the M&A strategy, develop the criteria which a potential partner should meet, perform the due diligence on a candidate, coordinate top management alignment and make the final deal. Their capabilities should lie in strategy and finance. They ensure that the integration fits the corporate strategy and will bring value to the company. This team could be permanent, reporting to the board of directors. In the period leading up to the deal, the overall coordination will rest here.

INTEGRATION TEAM

The integration team consists of operational and staff managers. Their interest is to ensure that a deal is made on a realistic basis. It is a role which is not common in many merger or acquisition cases these days. We are convinced that this integration team plays a role which is as important as the M&A team. An integration team will not be permanent, as it is always related to a specific integration case. The employees that are in it will vary, depending on the candidate.

The responsibility of this team is to act as a counterpart to or sparring partner for the M&A team. Their activities include the fit analysis and feasibility check: the 'Scan' part that is one of the deal-making activities.

We assume that the integration team will be led by the integration manager, who will be part of the M&A team.

THE IRRATIONAL SIDE OF DECISION MAKING

Peter Drucker made an excellent statement when he responded to an interviewer's question on why M&A seems to be the strategy of choice (Harari, 1997). 'I will tell you a secret', confided Drucker. 'Deal making beats working. Deal making is exciting and fun, and working is grubby. Running anything is primarily an enormous amount of grubby detail work and very little excitement, so deal making is kind of romantic, sexy. That's why you have deals that make no sense'.

Using a clear, structured and accepted approach will certainly help to increase the quality of decision making. Yet it turns out not to be enough. In several instances, we have come across the phenomenon that, even though a good formal approach was used, the decision-making process was steered by other predominantly irrational factors. Success also depends on the way you handle the process.

In this section we look into some of the factors that influence the decision-making process so that these can be taken into account. The quality of integration management realization will depend to a certain extent on the quality of the decision to go for it!

MANAGERIAL BIASES

In their article 'Desperately seeking synergy', Goold and Campbell (1998) present an interesting perspective on synergy and the failures often made while trying to realize it. They point out that this is partly due to the proneness of corporate executives to biases that distort their thinking. They continue to point out four biases: synergy bias, parenting bias, skills bias and upside bias.

Synergy bias refers to overestimation of the benefits and underestimation of the cost of synergy. In their 'obsession for synergy', executives make the wrong decisions. Goold and Campbell present examples of how this bias guides management behaviour in making the wrong decisions. Because of their strong belief that synergy should be created, the managers in the examples often overlooked the realities of their company or the market-place. They did not realize that synergy cannot be declared or forced to exist. Influenced by the parenting bias, they felt that they should be in control themselves, assuming that they had the right skills available. Unfortunately, their actions to 'create' synergy had unforeseen side-effects.

To improve the quality of decision making, managers should be aware of biases. Furthermore, Goold and Campbell advocate a disciplined approach to decision making, taking the possibility of biases into account beforehand. Finally, they suggest caution in the case of highly uncertain situations. Forums for sharing ideas are mentioned as an example of how to proceed cautiously. In doing this they implicitly refer to the company's culture and its impact on decision making. The more open the company culture is for experimenting with new ideas and views, the easier it will be to create awareness of these biases and deal with them.

TRAPS IN DECISION MAKING

There are yet more possible traps. As Hammond *et al.* (1998) stated: 'In making decisions, your own mind may be your worst enemy'. Their research-based view on understanding psychological traps in decision making presented a number of interesting pitfalls, which seem particularly attractive in relation to integration management ventures.

Anchoring trap

Hammond *et al.* describe the anchoring trap as 'the disproportionate weight the mind gives to the first information it receives, when considering a decision'. Perhaps you recognize the enthusiastic business unit manager who has seen a takeover opportunity and who is convinced, despite everything, that his gut-feeling is right. Or the cynical headquarters manager who cannot be convinced that defining specific integration benefits and planning accordingly will help realize these objectives.

Hammond *et al.* identify various ways to deal with this trap. One of them is consistent with our previously advocated approach, i.e. to use different perspectives to look at a business integration venture. Add to the M&A experts' visions the operational perspectives of those who will be responsible for realizing the planned benefits.

Another way to handle this trap, and thus increase the quality of decision making, is to seek information from a variety of sources. For example, we have argued in favour of using external experts to validate internal views, not only from a financial point of view but also from the operational and integrational viewpoints. Hammond *et al.* rightly argue that decision makers should be careful not to force their consultants in a certain direction when seeking their opinion.

Status quo trap

The status quo trap is the need that many decision makers have to continue the status quo. In the case of business integration, this means continuing with mergers and acquisitions and growing, without learning from the failures and mistakes. Or, alternatively, using one failed integration project as the reason to avoid other initiatives in the future.

This way of making decisions, often called 'human', can be countered in several ways, one of which is to start with clear objectives. This completely aligns with the approach that we have described, which underlines the need for integration objectives and a plan for the way in which they can be achieved. Another technique is to work through various integration options in a scenario analysis to counterbalance the status quo while evaluating the pros and cons. This should be done in terms of the present operations and the future strategic options. That is why a clear business vision is definitely required for a high-quality decision on business integration.

Sunk cost trap

In a parallel with what economists call 'sunk cost', Hammond *et al.* make us aware of the trap that, although we know rationally that earlier decisions (like sunk cost) are irrelevant to the present decision, they nevertheless play a role and might lead us to inappropriate decisions.

Here, the link with the company culture once again becomes very clear. If a company punishes the making of mistakes, it will be difficult for many managers to ignore a 'wrong' decision that they made in the past. They will not be willing to admit having made it, and will let it influence their future decisions.

Why don't managers whose integration projects failed tell all their colleagues and top management about it so that the whole company can learn from it and avoid making the same mistakes over and over again? It seems like the right thing to do – for your colleague or a manager in another company – but right now this is not something for *you* to do. Or is it?

Difficult as it is to deal with this behaviour, one of the ways to improve the quality of decision making is to allow for experimentation in the company and to reduce fear of failure. Hammond *et al.* also suggest involving in the decision-making process people who have not taken part in similar previous decisions.

Confirming evidence trap

Although this is a generic trap, business integration ventures and their failures seem to suffer enormously from falling into this trap. This trap means, of course, the seeking out of information that confirms our existing gut feeling or point of view and ignoring information that contradicts it.

To quote Hammond *et al.* again: 'There are two fundamental forces at work here. The first is our tendency to subconsciously decide what we want to do before we figure out why we want to do it. The second is our inclination to be more engaged by things we like than by things we dislike'.

In an earlier section in this chapter, we outlined several ways to deal with this trap. Hammond *et al.* suggest ensuring that you examine all the evidence – in our approach this is covered by extending the M&A process to include integration management issues. They also suggest letting someone play devil's advocate. We suggested involving the manager(s) who will have to realize the integration benefits in the decision-making process so that all the counter-arguments, risks etc. can be tabled and taken into account.

They even suggest being honest with yourself about your motives – good advice, but you would be optimistic to think that this by itself will work. Business integration failure rates suggest that more is needed.

Framing trap

Every experienced manager will recognize this trap. The way in which an issue is framed can profoundly affect the way decisions are made. In business integration, this also seems to happen when critical and full assessment of business integration ventures is seen as destructive, time-consuming and uncooperative. Questions such as 'how quickly can we integrate company Y into our division ABC?' ignore the issues of desirability and feasibility. More neutral phrasing certainly helps you to look into the issue more carefully and by doing so increases the chance of a higher quality decision.

Estimating and forecasting trap

This is another popular trap in business integration projects in both forms. The advocates of a certain business integration project will often suffer from overconfidence, whereas their opponents seem to suffer from seeing things too negatively. Earlier, we pointed out that the pessimists in this area seem to be right if the failure rate of 50–70 per cent is taken into account. In other words: too often overconfidence that the benefits will be realized is present, without any real basis.

Hammond *et al.* have presented several ways to improve this part of the decision-making process. They, like Goold and Campbell (1998), for example, suggest a strict approach for handling decision making, as we proposed in the previous sections.

Another option is to look at the extremes, such as developing a complete failure scenario as part of the integration management contribution to the deal-making phase.

Managers should state their assumptions as specifically as possible, and in this case actual statistics will help. In business integration terms, perform an extended due diligence investigation to identify real operational data and compare this, where possible, with performance data outside the company as well as checking internal consistency.

Groupthink

Along with the traps in decision making presented earlier, groups tend to have a special effect on the decision-making process. Let's consider the people who are generally involved in the phases prior to the deal.

We have the CEO and top management. They feel the pressure of the market-place, hear the shareholder expectations, see their rivals teaming up, read the press clippings about the concentration trends and M&A frenzy. They need to secure the company's continuity and may see integration as a way to secure it. On the other hand, we have the corporate M&A team, assisted by investment banks, corporate finance consultants and lawyers. They benefit from each deal they close and are eager to do so. Although experts in their own particular field, some of them have too limited a notion of the endurance, energy and work needed to make the targeted 'synergies' a reality in the integration phases.

Because of other factors, such as deadlines and confidentiality, no other parties are likely to be involved. So here we have a group of individuals, all with the same interests: closing the best deal possible. And the key word here is *close* – not *integrate, realize* or *make it work*.

So, in these circumstances, how do you make sure that you are making the right decision?

A lot of research has been done into the behaviour of groups. Janis (1971) introduced the word *groupthink* to address specific irrationalities in group dynamics. Social–psychological experiments show that powerful social pressures are exerted by the members of a cohesive group whenever a dissident begins to voice objections to a group consensus. Another common norm seems to be conforming to the group policies that have evolved, even if those policies are obviously having a negative effect on the group's performance. The group tends to conform to one state of mind, one opinion, and never to question it again. 'The more amiability and *esprit de corps* there is among the members of a policy-making inside group, the greater the danger that independent critical thinking will be replaced by groupthink, which is likely to result in irrational... actions directed against outside groups'.

Janis (1971) found eight symptoms of groupthink. These include a feeling of invulnerability. Members of the group tend to share an illusion of invulnerability that reassures them. They will think that there are no dangers ahead and are prepared to take extraordinary risks. It also causes them to ignore obvious warning signs. This is related to another symptom: the tendency of the group to develop rationalizations in order to minimize and reject warnings that in normal circumstances might lead them to re-evaluate the present course of action and develop alternatives. Members of groups also tend to apply direct pressure to those members who question the validity of the group's arguments to validate a policy. These members are violating group norms by trying to question the rationalizations made. This potentially conflicts with the illusion of invulnerability. Members are then falling into the status quo trap and will fiercely hold on to the feeling of security.

There are some recommendations which we think are valuable in pre-deal decision-making processes:

- The leader of the group should assign each member the role of critical evaluator and stress the importance that is given to the open discussion of arguments and doubts.
- The group should be given a neutral assignment at the beginning of a group effort to stimulate open inquiry and the discussion of as many options as possible.
- A control group that works simultaneously on the same assignment can act as a counterbalance.
- The group should invite external experts to meetings and to discuss important issues, and the experts should try to challenge the group's assumptions.
- Enough time and consideration should be given to alternative scenarios and the warning signs from the other organizations involved.
- While discussing solutions for feasibility and consequences, the group should split up and brainstorm under different discussion leaders and confront each other with the outcomes.

CONCLUSION

Taking into account all the biases and traps mentioned, it seems a miracle that proper decision making takes place at all. In this section, we have outlined the part of our Business Integration Approach that is linked to strategic decision making.

If these integration decisions are to be realized, they should be of high quality, i.e. they should be realistic and realizable. By being aware of the traps in this decision-making process and by using the approach advocated, managers will be in a better position to improve their decision making, which will benefit not only them but also the company(ies) involved as a whole.

4

INTEGRATION PROGRAMME MANAGEMENT

❖

INTRODUCTION

Having decided on the strategic intent of a business integration, as discussed in Chapter 3, we consider in this chapter the next challenge on the road to successful completion of the project – how to plan the realization in detail. The implementation plan that has been developed as part of the strategic intent phase will be the input for this planning.

Part I of this chapter presents current practices in planning and realization management. The results of business integration projects conclude this part. In Part II a number of the lessons learned, as perceived by the participants in our research, are presented. These are concerned with the best ways in which successful integration can be accomplished on time and within budget. Part III contains a framework for the planning and control of the realization of business integration projects. This framework is closely related to the development of programme management concepts, tools and techniques.

PART I: CURRENT PRACTICES IN INTEGRATION PROGRAMME MANAGEMENT

This part describes current practices in the planning and control of the realization of business integration endeavours. The integration strategy is also discussed. Aspects such as phasing, speed and priorities will be described. The section on integration organization (pp. 77–79) contains a description of which groups play an important role in the integration organizations of the participating companies. Furthermore, the way in which decisions are made will be discussed. In the section on integration planning (pp. 79–81), the various components of integration plans are presented. Other topics include the realization of changes in the operating models and the final results (success) of the integration processes of our research participants.

INTEGRATION STRATEGY

In this section, special attention is paid to existing practices regarding the overall integration strategy, phasing and integration speed. The participating companies have used various strategies in realizing their integration objectives.

OVERALL INTEGRATION STRATEGY

Several companies – especially those with full integration projects – defined an explicit integration strategy before they started the actual integration process. They knew what to do and how to do it. Here are some types of strategy that were frequently used.

Physical integration strategy

One common strategy was to put similar departments, processes or functions (production or marketing) together and re-engineer them, and then consolidate and finally optimize. Putting employees close together physically should help them to work together. Cultural integration has a better chance this way, and communication lines are very direct. However, this will involve relocation choices and new housing policies.

Blueprint strategy

Another strategy used has been to define in detail (blueprint) the new situation before starting up the actual integration process. Some even started by defining a new mission statement and developed their new business model from there. This strategy was used in the case of full integration in mergers.

One of the advantages of this strategy was the ease with which communication could take place because everything had been carefully planned. A downside is the time it takes before actual change takes place. And the longer it takes, the harder it gets.

Quick win strategy

Yet another strategy used – linked to the strategic intent of cost reduction – focused on achieving quick wins in performance improvement and reducing cost at the earliest possible moment, after which other integrational activities followed more slowly.

Cool-down strategy

One integration strategy started with a waiting period: a so-called cool-down strategy after the deal, postponing actual integration activities. Only after a certain period of getting to know one another were further integration activities started up.

In the initial phase many meetings between the management of the acquiring company and the acquired company took place in order to build trust between both management teams.

PHASING, PLANNING AND SCHEDULING

Most companies – regardless of the desired level of integration – thought about phasing the integration activities when they planned the integration. Some companies admitted though that they had not really phased their post-acquisition activities.

In several acquisitions external *ad hoc* factors (such as timing – completion before the start of a holiday season, for example) played an important role in the actual scheduling of integration activities.

In one acquisition case another method of phasing was found, which ran from analysis, awareness and planning to implementation. This company clearly planned the integration but used a cool-down strategy in order to ensure favourable integration circumstances. The awareness phase was needed to make people aware of the case for action, the way that the new organization would fit in and the business options that would be generated.

Two distinct alternatives can be found in the wide array of approaches used.

Cascade phasing

In several mergers, the phasing was linked to the job appointments at the different levels in the new company. The first phase – usually seen as the preparation phase – was completed when top management had been appointed. After that, using a cascading model for the process of filling in the vacant key management positions, the integration phases had been defined.

Each level of managers then planned the actions they would take. One phase could last as long as one to two years in complex mergers.

Systems implementation phasing

In the case of minimal integration, phasing is usually linked to the stepwise implementation of financial systems. This usually follows the path of making an inventory of the systems used, defining the set of system performance criteria and functionalities, and decision making about new systems, implementation and servicing. In addition, the business areas in which systems were replaced (headquarters, sales, logistics etc.) varied according to strategic intent and feasibility.

INTEGRATION SPEED

Integration speed varies throughout the integration phases. Usually, the speed of deal making is high because of confidentiality, competitive forces, negotiation strategies and adrenaline. Once the deal has been made, a more lengthy process of integration usually awaits.

Integration speed has been qualified by participants as slow to medium in mergers and internal integration and fast in acquisitions. 'Slow' varied from several (e.g. four) years to a year, whereas 'fast' was used for periods varying from several months to a year or two.

The complexity of full integration, as in a merger, is high and is bound to take more time to balance out than a 'straightforward' takeover of a small company which is then partially integrated into a division of an existing company.

Furthermore, in mergers almost everything is new. Both companies and their top managers have to find new ways of dealing with the changed setting. Decision making is one of those areas that takes time to get used to. In most acquisitions, it was clear who took the lead.

Quick or slow

Views on the topic of speed differ significantly. Some argue for a slow process, as part of the initial 'cool-down' phase of a full integration. This is in order to get a good understanding of possible synergies and to give people time to get to know one another. Others argue for a slow process in order to give employees sufficient time to deal with the consequences of the planned integration. This was the case, for example, in an internal integration process in which people needed to move to another country/region. In order to prepare them for this move, several employees were offered temporary accommodation in their new location so that they could get used to it without having to move the entire family at the outset.

In contrast, some vehemently advocate a quick '100/150 days' approach in which the essential integration has to take place. This in order to avoid too much uncertainty going on for too long, which also send the wrong signals to the market. Or in the words of one manager: 'You have got six months to do it, after that you can forget it'.

INTEGRATION ORGANIZATION

WHAT SOLUTIONS CAN BE DISTINGUISHED?

Planning the realization of an integration project raises the issue of who will manage the integration activities – do we need a dedicated integration organization? Resolving this issue requires a decision about who will be responsible and will plan and control these activities. The participating companies set up their integration organization in various basic ways.

1. *Board/management*
   In this alternative, responsibility for and coordination of the business integration process were assigned to top management. In the internal integration cases this meant regional management, including the HR director. Most of the mergers also opted for this solution, which placed the new top management in the driving seat of the whole integration process.

   In acquisition cases one Board member was often made responsible for realizing the post-acquisition integration. In several cases – and even in mergers – a decision was taken not to appoint a dedicated integration manager alongside the Board/management.

   Some companies that were active in acquisitions used the quality of top management as one of their criteria in selecting acquisition candidates. They assigned the responsibility for the realization of the planned integration to the existing top management of the acquired company. They felt that top management of the acquired company would know the market best, and by concentrating on alignment and interaction with these managers performance was optimized and unrest held to a minimum.
2. *Integration manager*
   In several cases a dedicated integration manager was appointed who was made responsible for realizing the planned integration. This was the case with acquisitions, but hardly ever with mergers, where the new top management wanted to manage the process themselves.

   This integration manager was seen as 'the spider in the web'. He or she managed all integration activities and was the integration champion. The integration manager needed many change management skills in order to be effective.

3. *Integration team(s)*
The third option was to set up an integration team which coordinated all integration realization activities. This solution was often found among the partial integration projects.
One company formed two kinds of team: value teams had to focus on finding the synergy benefits and the best practices of the two old companies and put together a plan to realize them. The other teams focused on making a list of actions for the actual integration, and later on formulated and executed an integration plan to handle these items.

4. *Combination*
Finally, in some cases an integration organization consisting of more than one tier was used. This usually implied a combination of one or more Board members, supported by an integration manager, who used integration teams to perform the realization activities.

Apart from these integration functions, additional ones have been used by the companies involved.

Steering Group

In those cases where an integration manager was active, he or she could report to the Board but also to a dedicated steering group, which was responsible for completing the integration process. The steering group consisted of responsible board members as well as key managers. This balanced the decision making in the integration process.

Integration office

Some companies set up project offices which acted like an 'integration headquarters'. Here, all the information concerning integration was processed, planning and control of the integration effort was managed and communication concerning the integration was centralized.

COMPOSITION OF THE INTEGRATION ORGANIZATION

Working together on the integration is part of cultural adaptation. Combined with the need for experience and knowledge of the old processes on both sides, teams generally consisted of personnel from both sides.

Integration teams were often staffed with functional managers, such as the HR Manager, Marketing Director or Sales Manager. In acquisitions, they were asked to identify integration options using their functional capabilities. Business process (operation) managers seem to have been used less often, although in a number of mergers it was these experts who were assessing synergy options in several core business processes.

In a few cases, setting up the integration organization was seen as an opportunity to put employees with high potential in positions where they could excel and were capable of shaping their own future.

Some companies stated that managing integration required dedicated capabilities, such as effective communication, planning and controlling complex projects, managing resistance and motivation. In a few cases – mergers and acquisitions – companies hired outside expertise to complement their own expertise and to assist in the realization of parts of the integration process.

DECISION MAKING

Political forces are strong in most integration processes, as many of our research participants experienced. They indicated that it is therefore important to agree on some ground rules for decision making with regard to integration. This means clarity about who decides what and who has to be informed.

Some organizations paid a great deal of attention to the procedures that were to be followed during the integration phase. For organizational changes that have an impact on employee numbers, the corporate Works Council, a body that looks after the interests of employees, must be involved and must give formal approval to the plans. Western European organizations are used to complex and detailed procedures in organizational change. Having those ready at the outset of an integration venture (social plan, involvement of the Works Council, appointment procedures for new managers) proved useful in managing the acceptance and support of employees.

An important issue that was presented by a small number of companies concerned the way in which the integration plan was accepted by the employees. Usually the Works Council was seen as the body for employee approval for this plan.

INTEGRATION PLAN

USE OF AN EXPLICIT PLAN

One third of the companies in this study did not have an integration plan! Those organizations that aimed for minimal integration did not use a formal plan, whereas most full integration projects were using a plan.

There was one case of full integration in which the company thought that an integration plan was unnecessary. Departments were simply housed together, assuming that this would be enough to achieve integration. Not surprisingly, not much came out of it.

When partial integration was aimed for, most companies used some kind of plan. This decision seems to depend on the size and fit of the acquired company.

A few companies implemented integration plans that had been used in previous integration projects. This was helpful to the extent that the 'old' plans still matched current circumstances. It was recognized that these plans needed adaptation if they were to be effective.

Plan development seems to have started mostly after the deal was done or after the letter of intent was signed.

PLAN ELEMENTS

Most companies that used a plan included at least the following elements.

Objectives

Objectives can be defined as a description of the required outcomes. The way the objectives were formulated varied significantly. Some used broad definitions, such as 'a significant increase in sales', whereas others were more specific: '10 per cent increase in market share in the next two years'. The companies that used broad definitions could not assess whether the integration was going according to plan, and hence they could not manage it effectively. Most objectives, however – apart from desired synergy – were of a financial nature, even for those companies that carefully planned their integration.

Phasing

Phasing can be defined as a description of the various stages or phases that the integration process will go through. Most companies – independent of the level of integration – had thought about this when planning the integration. However, several admitted that they had not really phased the post-acquisition activities. The scope and end result of each phase were not defined in many cases. This left the companies unable to measure or manage progress.

'Blueprint business model'

A blueprint business model can be defined as a description of the required operational situation once the integration project is finished. Some companies – especially those that were going for full integration via a merger – had made detailed designs. They discovered that this was very useful from a communication perspective. In reality, the very detailed designs had to be adjusted during the integration process to fit emerging needs. This part of the plan often contained a more detailed description of the new location when a relocation was required.

Activities

Integration activities can be defined as a description of the activities that have to be performed in order to achieve the integration objectives.

The appointment of top management, cultural issues, a social plan and communication were among the most common elements encountered in the study.

Integration organization

The integration organization can be defined as a description of the people who performed integration activities and the way in which they were organized.

Budget

The integration budget can be defined as a description of the budget needed to accomplish the integration objectives as a part of some plan. Many did not specifically allocate a budget for the realization of the integration project. Costs found their way into various parts of the profit and loss accounts, which made it difficult to trace the total integration cost.

PRACTICES IN REALIZING OPERATING MODEL CHANGES

INTRODUCTION

In this study a number of practices regarding the realization of operating model changes were collected. These will be presented in this section as an indication of the integration that must be planned and controlled in the realization of business integration.

During the integration realization, the operating models of the companies involved will change to a certain extent – in the case of full integration a dramatic change in the operating model is required (Figure 4.1). But this can also occur with partial integration.

In a very small number of situations almost no change in the operating model was implemented, related to the fact that only minimal integration was aimed for. In one case, a merger was planned but not fully realized, which could be seen from the almost non-existent changes in the operating model.

In this section, some of the experiences of companies with specific operating model changes will be presented using the model described below.

BUSINESS PROCESSES

Business integration cannot be done without a certain amount of change in the business processes of the companies involved in our study. The amount of change depended to a large extent on the required level of integration.

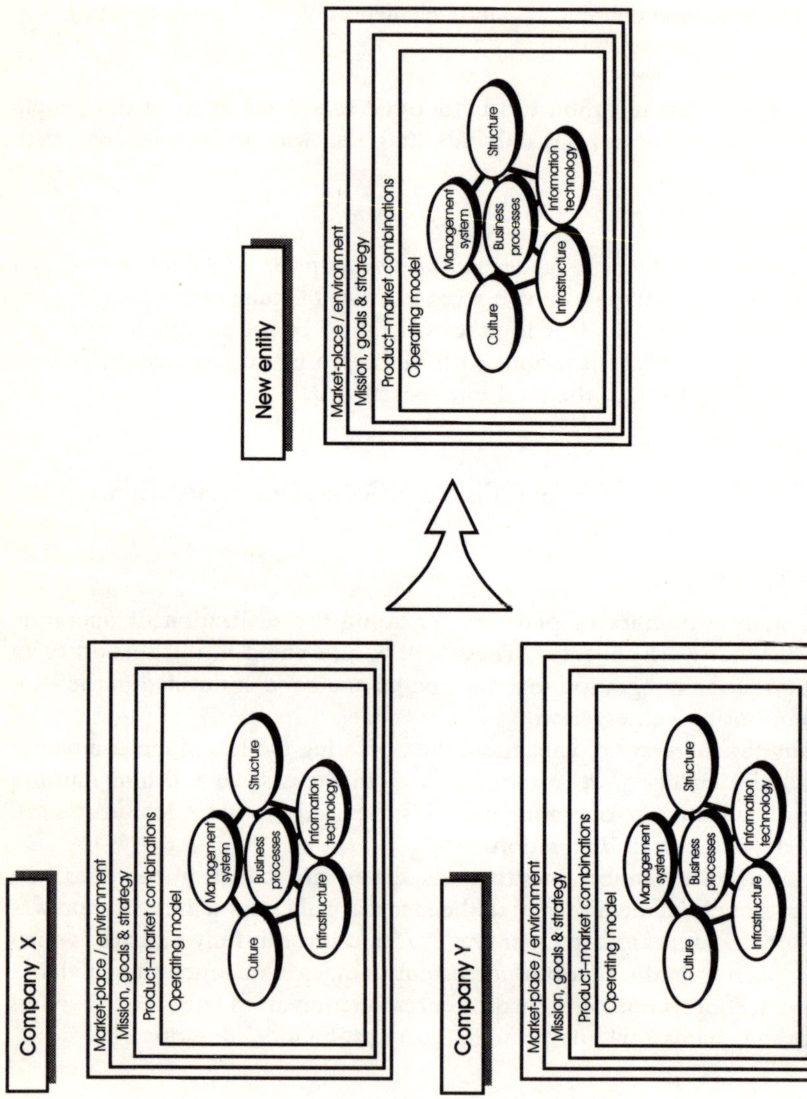

Figure 4.1 Merging two business models generates specific issues.

Full integration created the biggest challenge because the assumed similarities between companies sometimes disappeared when business processes were closely analysed.

Decisions had to be made about how to handle these process integrations. Some chose new process definitions, whereas others tried to learn from each other first and then select the 'best option'. These decisions were – at least partly – driven by the strategic intent.

One company set up eight teams to look into the current situations and define the required business processes. This, of course, was done in relation to the other aspects of the operating model, such as the organizational structure, the supporting information systems and so on.

Most business process changes were made in:

- logistics
- purchasing
- operations
- marketing
- sales
- research and development
- finance
- information management

Realizing partial integration posed a different challenge with regard to changing business processes. What kind of integration was aimed for? Should one or more core business processes be shared, or would the back office processes have to be shared with the acquired company? The latter was the case in the majority of partial integration projects. Cost reductions aimed for were realized by sharing overheads. Usually, these integrations included sharing the same financial process in order to ensure prompt and standardized financial reporting, but the integration of core business processes such as sales and marketing, purchasing, and research and development also took place.

Changes due to minimal integration strategies seemed to be limited to one or two processes, one being finance management. In these cases prompt and standardized financial reporting was seen as critical and was always implemented in one way or another. In another minimal integration case, purchasing was shared due to the significant financial advantages this generated.

ORGANIZATIONAL STRUCTURE

Logically, full integration leads to adaptation of the organizational structure of the entities involved. Depending on the integration objectives and other (sometimes practical) issues departments were integrated into new organizational units. This usually implied that the existing entities were placed inside a new organizational structure – for example a new business unit.

The timing of this part of the integration varied in the various projects and even within an integration process. In one case, it turned out not to be very practical to integrate two support departments before they migrated to a single shared information system.

The level of integration also varied between the various organizational units. In several cases, despite the fact that it was decided to go for full integration, a number of departments remained more or less separate, sometimes for geographical reasons (they were located too far apart to make it useful to physically integrate them) and sometimes for cultural reasons.

Partial integration cases showed a wide range of options, from limited structural change (positioning the acquired company as a member of an existing division) to large adaptations in the organizational structure of the acquired organization, for example via back office integration while leaving the front office separate.

In minimal integration projects the organizational structure was left as it was for the reasons stated previously. An issue that usually came about had to do with the reporting lines from the acquired company to the Board of the new parent company. This was often solved by appointing a Board member with responsibility for the company involved.

MANAGEMENT SYSTEMS

Changing the management systems depended, among other things, on the integration objectives and controls that were put in place. Control almost always meant financial control. It also depended on the availability of an explicit integration plan. Without such a plan, changing the management systems was not a logical option to choose.

Full integration projects required many adjustments to the available management systems. The majority of these systems were still financial. Although often recognized as very important, not much attention was given to a full implementation of these systems during these integration projects. A lot of time was spent on integrating labour terms and conditions, but not much on aligning the management systems. The same holds true for the partial integration projects.

Minimal integration, if this is more than just a financial link between parent and child companies, needed certain management systems. One company tried to implement 'standardized' management systems that it thought would enhance performance in the child companies. This did not have the expected results. Since they wanted more than just a financial link, certain exchanges between parent and child and between child companies were necessary. They changed tactics and moved from the introduction of formal standardized systems to stimulating a mutual consultative approach, in which child companies could learn from each other and from the parent company. This led to a more successful method of exchanging expertise and a growing understanding of best practice in many areas.

IT SYSTEMS

IT is always present in the top three topics that managers worry about. IT systems played a key role in business integration projects because – apart from the physical integration – they enabled information integration, or were at least supposed to do so. Furthermore, IT systems were often a serious cost. Finally, most IT systems had the ability to utterly frustrate business processes by not functioning well and not delivering the required information.

Even in those cases where minimal integration was wanted and only financial processes were shared, information systems were the most important tool for realizing this.

In most partial integration projects, and also those in which the newly acquired company was given a lot of independence, information systems were usually forced upon the acquired company by the acquiring organization. Some major problems had to be dealt with when, for example, the company acquired a business which had an IT system that was focused on a different product. This required the definition and implementation of a whole new system before integration at IT level could be accomplished.

In full integration processes the information systems played an even more important role. One company indicated that one of the reasons for merging was the ability (for the merged company) to acquire state-of-the-art information systems, something that as standalone companies they would not have been able to fund. These systems in turn must lead to a better grip on business processes and lead to performance improvements and cost reduction.

Information systems, being the enabler of integration that they are, nevertheless became a hindrance to full integration in some cases. Because of the incompatibility of the information systems used, it turned out to be almost impossible to effectively integrate the administrative processes. A new system had to be implemented before effective integration was possible.

And, as one company underlined, selecting information systems has serious implications. If one or more of the systems of one of the merging partners is selected, this might lead to certain IT staff leaving, which in turn means that legacy systems (bespoke software) can no longer be effectively maintained, with all the serious business risks attached to such a situation.

In one internal integration project, the implementation of an ERP package was used as a driver for integration. Both entities, which had been separate before the internal integration took place, were thinking about moving to a new version of the ERP package involved. In order to ensure that a joint method of working was designed, a new implementation was prepared. Selecting one of the existing systems was not a workable solution because each system was built around the old organization and therefore did not match the current business requirements of the newly integrated business.

INFRASTRUCTURE

One hot topic in many mergers is the location of the new company's headquarters. The obvious symbolic function of the company HQ has led several companies to select a new location which was not occupied by either company before the merger.

Another very hot topic linked to this is the relocation of the place of work for employees. Changes in the workplace hit employees very hard. A number of companies went through careful exercises in which they calculated the average distance for employees to their workplace. Locations were selected based on the best score on minimal average distance for employees involved.

In all infrastructure issues, geography plays an important role. When, for example, a European company acquires an Australian company, nobody will start to worry about moving people into one location or headquarters. But an entirely different situation arises when a company is acquired within the borders of a nation with cost reduction as one of the main drivers.

In our research, minimal integration cases never caused HQ or other relocation problems, for obvious reasons.

Partial integration projects had to deal with these location issues, and again showed a wide spectrum of ways of dealing with this. Several companies maintained current HQ locations, whereas others opted for a new HQ.

Full integration mostly posed the issue of a new HQ, one reason being the cost reduction that could be achieved by physically integrating both companies. Other reasons were to avoid a feeling of dominance and to break with the past.

In internal integration projects a lot of attention was given to the relocation of the HQ. This was a very sensitive issue, particularly because this often implied crossing national borders (and all that is related to that: language, culture, legal guidelines, terms and conditions etc.). Sometimes a choice like this led to a significant loss of employees, because in the end they did not want to move or travel so much every day to their HQ-bound job.

In one merger, two companies moved into the HQ of one of the companies and the other HQ was closed. Since this HQ was quite close to the other HQ no measures were taken to deal with possible problems.

In several others a completely new HQ was built. One company used the construction of its new HQ as a symbol of the growing integration and informed its employees about construction progress, showing pictures of it in the integration magazine. Another selected a location for the new HQ halfway between the existing HQs.

However, as stated above, it was not only the location of the HQ that was an issue. The locations of other offices, production facilities, distribution centres etc. were carefully calculated in order to optimize travelling time to work for as many employees as possible.

In yet another case, optimizing the organization implied moving several smaller offices into a single bigger one. This had the benefit of starting afresh in a new building and by doing so avoided the impression that one company had moved in on the other.

RESULTS

Every business integration project starts with (often implicit) objectives. Looking back, the participants in our study gave their views on how much had been achieved. It should be remembered that this was at an early stage for some projects because we carried out the study when the companies were in the middle of their integration project.

Overview

Results are linked to ambition: what did the companies set out to achieve? Those who opted for minimal integration seem to be satisfied at this point. The financial performance of their acquisitions is seen as satisfactory, and in one case an exchange of capabilities had begun, which was seen as important and satisfactory.

The companies that realized partial integration present a more diverse picture. Forty per cent of the participating companies are very positive about the results of the integration process. This is linked directly to the financial performance of the acquired company. The other 60 per cent state that they are either moderately positive or negative. The financial performance in these cases is seen as positive, but negative side-effects have surfaced and damaged the integration results.

Some of these negative side-effects are:

- loss of key employees/managers
- disappointment with the acquired organization
- inadequate realization of integration plans
- lack of sufficient structure in the integration process resulting in sub-optimal performance in the acquired company

Looking back on the full integration projects, of which a number are still under way, results in a mixed picture.

Approximately 30 per cent are (very) positive about the results achieved. This implies that they have realized cost reductions, greater financial means for further development and increased availability of core capabilities. But even these companies identify some serious issues regarding the loss of employees, disappointing growth in sub-sectors and less capable management.

Of the remaining companies, only one is wholly negative about the outcomes of the merger, which is seen as a failed integration. The hoped-for synergy, exchange of capabilities and cultural integration have not come about.

The other companies present a picture in which some important results have certainly been achieved, often in cost reduction. But they also see a number of downsides, such as the loss of key staff, an imbalance in organizational mixture, and higher costs than planned.

Integration costs

Not many of the participating companies could present a complete picture of the integration costs. Only a few were convinced that the integration costs were within the planned budget.

Some stated very openly that they really did not know what the total integration costs over the years were. And one company indicated that the actual integration cost would have been at least twice the original budget.

PART II: BEST PRACTICES IN INTEGRATION PROGRAMME MANAGEMENT

INTRODUCTION

Based on their integration experiences, all participants were asked to present their lessons learned regarding the integration processes and by doing so help to design best practices in the area of Integration Programme Management.

In defining these best practices, the focus has been on the implementation part of business integration. Therefore, in the following sections, we present the defined best practices for:

- planning
- controlling integration realization
- decision making
- integration organization
- learning from integration experience

PLANNING

CENTRALIZED AND FORMAL PLAN

One best practice concerns the need for a centralized and formal integration plan. Even those who planned their integration up to a certain level concluded that this was not good enough. The quality of the integration plan defines, to a large extent, the way in which the integration process can be managed. Serious effort should be put into defining this plan, using as much (external) expertise as possible.

DETAILED INTEGRATION PLAN

The successful management of business integration requires an activity plan which needs to be realized in order to achieve the defined integration outcomes. This best practice also underlines the importance of the various components of the plan.

CLEAR INTEGRATION OBJECTIVES

The integration objectives, i.e. the outcomes that should be achieved as a consequence of the planned business integration, should be clearly defined.

By doing so these objectives can be communicated effectively. These should be easy to understand for those concerned and should also be realizable. Setting clear and measurable objectives enables employees to focus their energy on supporting activities. It also guides priority setting for a number of issues like resource allocation.

Therefore top management should be absolutely clear about the results that need to be achieved to realize the planned business integration project and how these will be measured.

PRIORITIZED INTEGRATION BENEFITS ACTIONS

Although often overestimated, integration benefits can only be effectively achieved by prioritizing the actions that employees must realize to achieve these benefits. It is of the utmost importance to ensure that those actions that really lead to the creation of added value get the highest priority and are carried out accordingly.

Directly linked to this prioritizing of actions is the implementation of a monitoring mechanism that allows the integrators to keep track of the results of these actions and compare them with the planned outcomes. Only in this way can it be ensured that the planned benefits become reality.

Prioritizing benefits is seen as part of managing the soft side because, although many benefits may be defined in financial terms, the realization of these benefits can only be achieved by people changing their behaviour to include these objectives. The need, the hierarchy and the sequence should therefore be clearly understood by those who have to realize these benefits if the required behaviour change is to be realized.

PLAN THE MANAGEMENT OF EMOTIONS

Some argued that the management of the emotional (or irrational) parts of integration processes should be explicitly incorporated into the planning. Integration processes are by definition full of emotion (see also Chapter 5) which can become a serious hindrance and also cause a lot of unnecessary discomfort. The integration plan should define actions to better deal with the irrational component of integration.

Along the lines of emotion management, a lesson learned here was that it is better to plan to deal with these 'me issues' first, because otherwise they will hinder the process significantly.

PLAN INFORMAL MEETINGS

Another lesson learned in this group regarded the planning of informal internal exchange. Although it seems to be a contradiction in terms, the lesson here is that planning almost always defines formal activities. And yet, in these emotional and complex integration processes time is needed to better understand the 'others'. Creating informal meetings will help to support this.

PLAN THE 'AFTER EFFECT'

The need to plan for the 'after effect' of a full integration process, i.e. the cultural integration, was broadly recognized. Every integration project has a certain completion time which in general will be shorter than the time that is actually needed to completely integrate the cultures of two companies. Therefore it is important to plan for these activities even after the integration project has been closed down.

PLAN FOR HIGH-SPEED INTEGRATION

Several companies identified the need to plan for a quick integration, assuming that if the integration has not been realized within three to six months, the benefits would disapear.

The longer it takes to realize integration benefits, the harder it gets. Also, the longer it takes, the higher the integration benefits need to be. Delaying the financial integration benefits results in a lower NPV (net present value), whereas the integration premium has already been paid.

Speed, decisiveness and consistency reduce the time and possibilities for personnel to become more uncertain, for the competition to react, and for market focus to slide away. This does not mean that the integration plan should be rigid, though: there has to be a certain amount of flexibility to make use of opportunities that arise during the integration. This can be ensured by decisive, clear and consistent management, rather than detailed planning and rigid control.

PLAN FOR THE FIRST 100 DAYS

There is a rule of thumb in integration management that says 'half the value is captured in the first half year'. The concept of planning for the first 100 days has been used to create a sense of urgency and make the integration effort go faster. It has already proven its success.

By setting a deadline at a more or less symbolic number, a picture of what has to be achieved by that time can be communicated. The faster the new organization has achieved a certain level of change, the better are its chances of success in the rest of the process.

Some call this strategy a 'parachute jump' approach. There is only a limited window of opportunity for a parachute jumper to jump if she wants to land at a certain spot on the ground. Once she jumps, there is no way back. The same applies to integration. Management has to create a sense of urgency: if we don't do it now, and with all our heart, the window of opportunity will pass. Once the organization enters the first 100 days programme, everyone is focused on achieving a certain level of change. Having begun, there is no way back. Employees can feel the change and see that it works, which should generate fresh energy for the next stages.

The lessons learned in the partial integration processes confirmed the need for a formal and detailed integration plan.

PLAN FOR SYNERGY

Many people have concluded that synergy cannot be forced to happen. Yet if there is to be any synergy, one should plan for it. This implies focusing on those areas where synergy is most likely to be achieved. If these cannot be identified, serious doubts should be raised as to whether synergy can be achieved at all. A golden rule for achieving synergy is mutual respect and trust. Without these there will be no synergy.

The managers of minimal integration projects also concluded that they saw a need for a more detailed and explicit integration plan. They also underlined the lesson identified earlier that a quick integration process should be planned for.

PLAN A FAILURE SCENARIO

The companies involved also added the need to design a failure scenario so that the responsible managers will be able to deal effectively with the first signs of failure and will not be unnecessarily surprised. This would otherwise decrease their effectiveness to deal with these situations.

CONTROL THE INTEGRATION REALIZATION

Only the managers of the partial integration processes provided details of best practices in the management of the actual integration process.

MANAGE INTEGRATION FORMALLY

Several managers concluded that for a successful integration process formal management is required; much more than had been involved so far. This implies tight control of the integration progress. It also implies continued formal management of the integration until the integration objectives have been achieved.

REVIEW REGULARLY

However well planned, business integration projects will come across unforeseen situations, either inside or outside the company. In a highly volatile environment with heavy competition, in particular, it is impossible to plan everything ahead in detail.

Therefore it is important to frequently review the integration results and compare these with the original plan. This should lead to an updated version of the integration plan and to corrective actions, when necessary.

The review should also focus on the planned process or the way forward. This cannot be cast in stone in volatile environments with a high level of complexity, such as a cross-border merger.

Regular reviews help to increase control of the management of the soft side of business integration. They also help to understand what the real integration issues are, compared with those that were foreseen at the outset of the event.

CREATE MORE SUPPORT

Another best practice concerns the level of internal support within both companies for the integration plan. Getting sufficient support should be carefully managed because it enhances the effectiveness of the integration process significantly. This also implies the need to involve both companies, even when a small company is acquired by a large one.

PAY ATTENTION TO CUSTOMER RETENTION

In today's market-place it is very hard to expand market share. This is one of the reasons why companies buy other firms. Losing customers, for whatever reason, is one of the pitfalls of integration and can cause the very driver for integration to be less valuable. As was said earlier, personal concerns drive most employees during the integration period. With that internal focus, customers are often neglected.

One company integrated the sales department of the acquired company. Some of the old employees left. After the integration, customers would call and order articles from the acquired company's product portfolio or ask questions about it. But in the transition, experience and expertise were lost and no one paid any attention to securing it.

DECISION MAKING

In this area two almost opposite best practices were formulated. One comes from full integration projects: implement top-down decisions. Several participants, apparently out of frustration with too much compromise in the process, argue the case for a more top-down driven type of decision making. By so doing this ensures a consistent implementation of the vision at the various levels of the new company. The other element related to this is a quick decision-making process, which helps with the high integration speed mentioned before.

A different best practice comes from minimal integration processes. If local management (of an acquired company, for example) is to remain in place and have their company perform adequately, they need room to make their own decisions instead of being 'guided' (i.e. forced) by corporate decisions.

INTEGRATION ORGANIZATION

MAKE BUSINESS MANAGERS RESPONSIBLE FOR INTEGRATION

Defining clear integration objectives is not enough to ensure that they will be realized. Another key factor is to make line managers responsible for achieving these objectives. Those who are responsible for the newly integrated entity(ies) should be held accountable for achieving these desired outcomes.

It is considered best practice for business managers to be made responsible for realizing integration objectives.

APPOINT AN INTEGRATION MANAGER

If integration is to be taken seriously, it is not something that will just happen. Even when line management is made responsible, this is often not enough to ensure that the desired outcomes will be achieved. Running a newly integrated operation is complex and time-consuming, and at the same time a lot of change activities will have to be performed in order to ensure further progress towards the integration outcomes.

Having a dedicated integration manager, as part of the managing the soft side of business integration, is seen as best practice to improve the management of the soft side of business integration.

Managing a going concern effectively does not qualify a manager for the position of integration manager. More qualities are needed. The ideal integration manager is a people manager, because at heart that is what integration is all about.

INTEGRATION CAPABILITIES

A successful acquisition requires certain integration capabilities in the organization that is acquiring a company (and also at the acquired company). It must be ensured that those capabilities are available before the actual integration is started. These capabilities should be available inside the company or should be hired from consulting companies that have integration management capabilities. By this we do not mean the functional expertise needed in the deal phase, such as corporate finance or legal or fiscal expertise, but actual integration management capabilities.

WORKS COUNCIL INVOLVEMENT

In a number of countries – certainly in The Netherlands – the Works Council plays an important role in the formal acceptance process of the integration in a company.

When two entities merge, a solution has to be found for both Works Councils. It is seen as best practice to integrate these councils as soon as possible to form a new joint Works Council. This will help to ensure that integration is supported from this side as well.

LEARNING FROM INTEGRATION EXPERIENCE

Finally in this set of best practices, some others were defined based on hard lessons in this area.

USE AVAILABLE EXPERTISE

Before starting an integration venture, a lot of effort should be put into making experience from inside and outside the company available to those who will be involved in one part or another of the integration process. Reinventing the wheel should be prevented, because the mistakes made so far have been very costly in both financial and people terms. Ideally, this should take place before an integration process is started.

TRANSLATE LEARNING INTO APPROACH

The best way for a company to learn from integration efforts is to translate these into a corporate approach, which can then be used throughout the company. This of course implies that, as soon as new experience is gathered, it should be evaluated and used to upgrade the integration approach. This topic will be further addressed in Chapter 5.

CONCLUSION

Although the participating companies can be seen as having some or a lot of experience with business integration, most of them were convinced that they could significantly improve their planning and control of the realization of business integration ventures. They identified many best practices during the interviews which can be very valuable if they are used as part of an overall approach. Therefore, in Part III of this chapter we will present a framework for integration programme management, taking these best practices into account.

PART III: FRAMEWORK FOR INTEGRATION PROGRAMME MANAGEMENT

INTRODUCTION

In this final part of the chapter, a framework to manage the integration process will be presented (Figure 4.2).

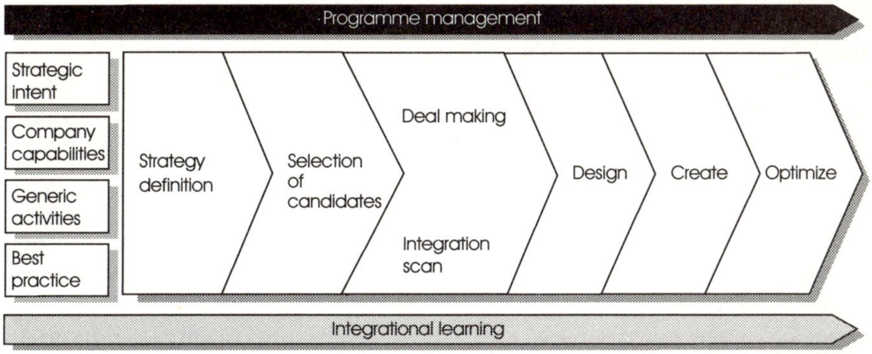

Figure 4.2 The Business Integration Approach.

One of the keys to successful integration is the design and use of an integrated framework for the planning and control of all integration activities. Since realization of the integration objectives almost always implies a series of activities and projects, a framework choice has to be made.

PROGRAMME OR PROJECT?

The key to understanding the difference between a programme and a project lies in the specificity of the outcome. A project has a clearly defined result at a certain predefined point in time; for example, a new office will be opened on 1 August next year.

A programme, e.g. one which will have to lead to a new culture, certainly has a required outcome. The exact point in time will be difficult to assess in advance (when will the culture be 'ready'?). A level of subjectivity will also play a role (some might consider the new culture to be really customer-focused, whereas others still have their doubts).

In other words, projects lead to predefined results, whereas a programme is focused on the achievement of a set of objectives. Wijnen (1994) has illustrated these differences. He underscores the difference between a programme and a megaproject; the latter, although extremely complex, is still focused on a predefined specific result. He also points out the difference between a programme and a multi-project situation. In this, a series of projects without relevant coherence must be realized by a certain organization. The only link here is the fact that all these projects must be performed by one company. Wijnen refers to typical multi-project organizations such as engineering companies, architects and IT departments.

INTEGRATION PROGRAMME

If the complexity is too high and the overall objectives are vague, programme management can be a very helpful tool. Certainly in these cases, where the entities involved are autonomous and the desired integration is no longer automatic, programme management offers an attractive solution, according to Wijnen (1994).

Integration objectives

In almost all cases of business integration, an integration programme is called for. Even in cases where minimal integration is to be achieved, at least some of the outcomes cannot be pinpointed in time. Take the case in which the exchange of best practice between the managements of various subsidiaries in one region is a desired outcome. This is an important objective, but not a result that can be guaranteed to happen within five months after closing an acquisition deal. Therefore, integration requires a programme approach.

Integrated approach

Integration projects have become known as being complex, high-risk, partly irrational and difficult to manage, and the stakes are often very high. The only effective way to achieve success is to carefully plan and control all the integration activities in an integrated manner. Only then is it possible to handle the underlying relationships and influences effectively.

Multiple activities and projects

The complexity of full integration projects such as mergers and internal integrations, but also of partial integration exercises, is such that many activities and projects will have to be performed simultaneously. This requires an insight into the objectives that they have to contribute to.

Subjectivity

Mergers, acquisitions and internal integrations are known to have a high emotional level from the start. A top manager 'believes' in this opportunity, which 'must be considered' strategic for one or two companies. Too often the rationale for a business integration venture is called synergy, but is not traceable in the way we described in Chapter 3, based on Sirower (1997). Therefore, to a certain extent, subjectivity plays a role. Since the realization of this complex change process will take a certain time and many industries have a volatile character, only part of the vision can be defined in detail in advance. Part of it will have to be changed or updated during the integration, as conditions surrounding the programme change. Programme management offers a way to handle the subjectivity of integration.

This framework will be presented in the following sections. The section on integration programmes (pp. 99–104) argues the case for the programme management approach. The section on the integration programme planning (pp. 104–108) deals with the planning of an integration programme, while the section on integration programme organization (pp. 108–113) discusses the ways in which the people involved in the programme can be organized.

INTEGRATION PROGRAMME

In order to get a better understanding of what an integration programme is, a definition (based on Wijnen, 1994) will be presented here. Furthermore, several aspects, such as its objectives, its structure and the management of an integration programme will be addressed.

DEFINITION

An integration programme is defined as a coherent set of important, objective-driven integration actions, consisting of improvisations, routines, activities and (result-driven) projects, which is unique and finite but which in terms of results has an unpredictable end.

The key elements can be explained as follows.

- *Coherence*: it is vital that all integration activities are part of an overall scheme which is optimized using various perspectives; without coherence, effectiveness and efficiency are lost. More seriously, operational reliability is threatened by uncontrolled change activities, often resulting in decreasing performance.
- *Objective-driven*: all effort is focused on realizing the defined integration objectives.
- *Actions*: necessary to realize the integration objectives, such as one-off improvisations, changing routines and projects with clearly defined results.

- *Unique*: each integration programme is unique because it combines certain people with certain organizations at a certain point in time.
- *Finite*: each integration programme has a limited duration (even if this is several years) as opposed to the continuity drive of each company; a programme ends at a definite point in time, although at the start one cannot state specifically with which results.

Integration programme management is defined as managing an integration programme.

One of the key roles here is leading: having the integration vision, communicating this to the organizational entities involved, and ensuring that the vision becomes reality. Another key role is planning the realization, which also requires control as part of the realization.

Giving directions in the realization process is also an important part of integration programme management because it helps to deal with the changing everyday realities and the complexities of changing companies and people.

INTEGRATION PROGRAMME OBJECTIVES

Integration programme objectives cannot all be so-called 'smart' objectives, that is, specific, measurable, actionable, realistic and time-bound. As has been argued before, defining the integration objectives is partly a visionary activity which will sometimes lead to broad objectives that need further elaboration over time.

It is therefore critical to describe the integration objectives as realistically as possible. This includes the definition of the criteria which will be used in the future to decide whether or not the activities will contribute to the realization of the integration.

It is also important to clearly define the scope of the integration programme: what does and what does not belong to the integration programme? Running the ongoing business should not be made part of the integration programme. This is necessary to avoid the integration programme being used as an excuse for underperformance.

On the other hand, planning what was called the 'after effect' in Part II of this chapter identified the need to plan for post-integration programme activities in certain areas, such as cultural integration in a full integration project. Cultural differences will not completely disappear even after a three-year integration programme. Therefore this needs to be addressed as part of the closing down stage.

The relationship between the integration programme and other change projects should be made clear at the start, both for projects inside the company(ies) involved and for those involving external organizations.

INTEGRATION PROGRAMME STRUCTURE

Once the integration objectives have been outlined, it becomes important to structure these objectives, i.e. to group the different parts (activities, projects etc.) into logical, controllable and objective-driven clusters.

So-called objectives–activities networks are used to set priorities and ensure the manageability of the whole venture (see Figure 4.3).

In the objectives–activities network, each cluster has its own internal coherence. Each cluster should have as few interfaces with other clusters as possible. Wijnen (1994) states that a minimum of two and a maximum of seven clusters is a good rule of thumb. Many types of cluster can be identified, depending on the criteria used, such as organization-focused, sequential, results-driven, functional, financial, market-driven, geographic or mixed. Prioritization of integration objectives can now be done in a planned way, providing a realization framework at the same time.

INTEGRATION PROGRAMME PERFORMANCE CRITERIA

In order to manage an integration programme effectively, management criteria are needed. We will use the following performance criteria: speed, feasibility, efficiency, flexibility and effectiveness, as defined by Wijnen (1994).

1. *Integration speed*
   With this criterion integration programme management must be able to measure and judge when a programme activity will deliver the desired contribution. This information should help to assess the required duration of the various stages of the integration programme.

   Based on the outcomes of the study and on our experience, we propose a speed for the realization phase such that, within a reasonable time (e.g. six months), a basic level of integration is achieved. After that, depending on the strategic intent, the complexities of optimizing the integration may take much longer.

   We also advise using the intermediate results linked to so-called planning platforms. This means that the integration objectives are broken down into intermediate results, which are linked to a certain phase of realization of the business integration programme. In Figure 4.4 these platforms are shown in relation to the planned duration of the integration programme.
2. *Feasibility*
   This criterion should allow integration programme management to assess the likelihood that a desired activity will deliver its desired contribution. The more likely it is that an activity will deliver, the higher the priority it should have.

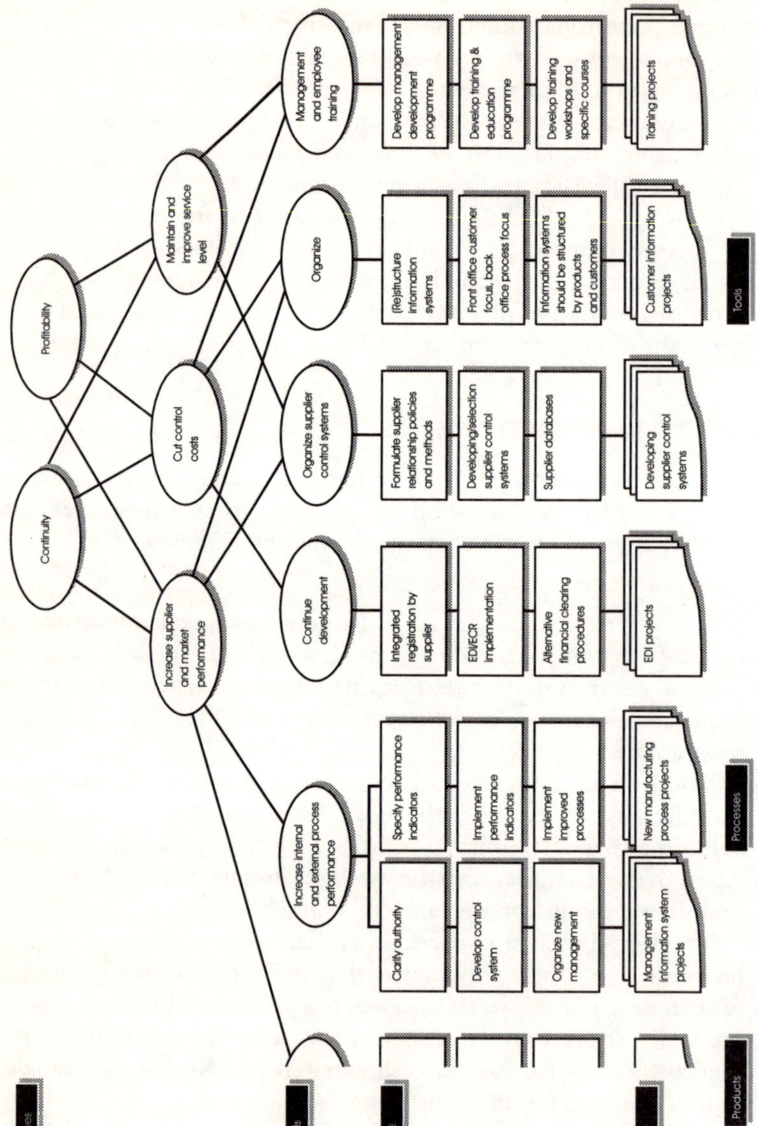

Figure 4.3 Objectives–activities network.

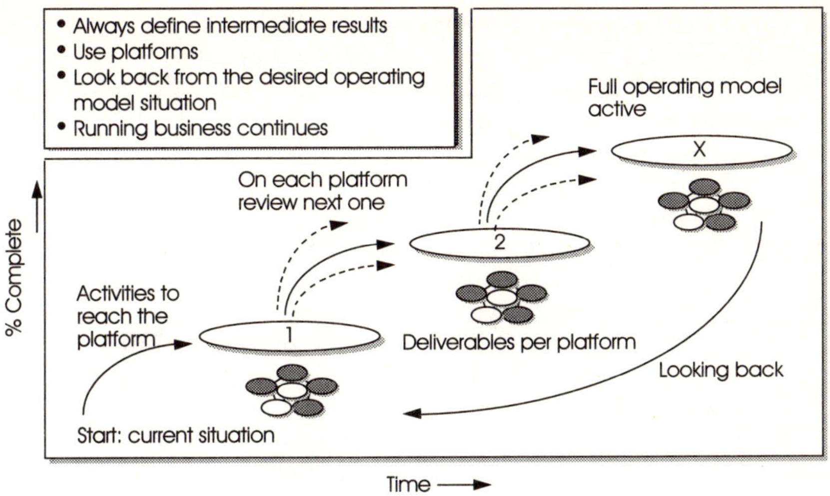

Figure 4.4 The use of implementation platforms.

(a) *Risk analysis*
In basic integration programme management, an integration risk analysis is made beforehand. In this way, risks can be dealt with in an effective way. By doing this in advance, the time needed to react is much smaller and the action more rational.

(b) *Integration programme failure scenario*
In such complex ventures as integrations, we also propose that a failure scenario is designed. This scenario should encompass external developments unforeseen when the deal was closed, counter-reactions from competitors or customers, synergies that suddenly disappear, conditions that make it impossible to realize combination benefits, unrest and resistance beyond expectation.

Scenario making can produce valuable contributions to effective integration management. By thinking about the scenarios, those involved make a mental note of the potential dangers of integration. Later on in the integration process, they will be more alert to the early warning signs of problems. If these problems have been thought about before they arise, employees will be less surprised and better prepared.

(c) *Ensuring running business*
One of the main risks of starting an integration process is that a lot of attention is drawn away from day-to-day operations and moved to the integration programme. This may lead to

faltering business performance and consequently to decreasing means for realizing the integration programme.

Although continuing to run the business is not seen as part of the integration programme, experience shows that continuity of these business operations is essential. Because of decreasing performance, management might be forced into a position where they will have to make choices about where to use their scarce resources, both financial and human. By taking the best employees away from running the business and putting them into the integration programme, day-to-day business will suffer. This impact will have to be monitored in order to avoid throwing the baby out with the bathwater.

3. *Efficiency*

   This criterion allows integration programme management to evaluate the financial value of the programme's activities in relation to each other. Some might be more cost-effective than others. However, this is difficult to do because in many cases programme activities are unique and therefore difficult to judge

4. *Flexibility*

   This criterion identifies how easy it is for integration programme management to change the planned activity, which can also imply stopping the activity or changing its nature.

   In particular, in hyper-competitive markets with high rates of change, flexibility is crucial, but any integration programme should have a certain degree of flexibility to deal with unforeseen reactions inside the company(ies) involved.

5. *Effectiveness*

   Using this criterion, the integration programme management must be able to measure the extent to which the programme activities will contribute to the realization of the defined integration objectives.

   If synergy is an objective, then its effectiveness should be tested as part of the performance. As identified earlier, synergy objectives, areas and activities should be made explicit and be part of the integration programme structure. Here, an effectiveness test should take place before irrational expectations that will result in disappointments and lower performance arise.

INTEGRATION PROGRAMME DEFINITION

When should an integration programme be developed? As we have argued in Chapter 3, we are convinced that a basic implementation programme outline

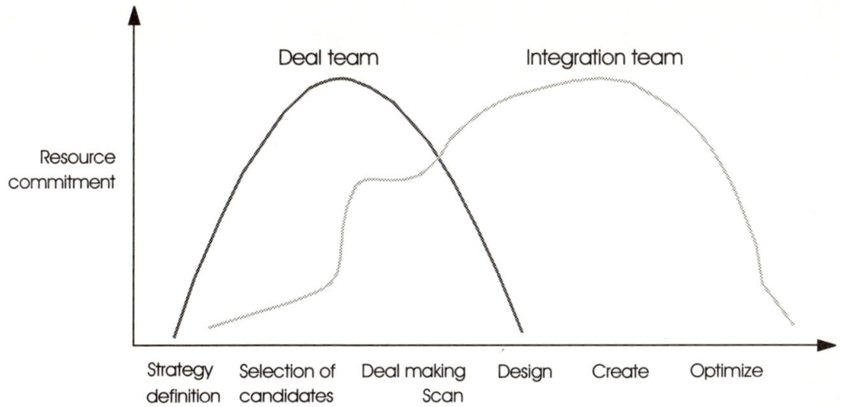

Figure 4.5 Staff planning during the integration process.

is needed in the decision-making phase for a merger, acquisition or internal integration. Only when armed with this information, can a balanced decision be made as to whether or not to go ahead with the intended business integration.

Thus the first outlines of an integration programme should be drawn up during the deal-making phase (Figure 4.5).

The decision makers for the integration programme will have to be the same as those that decide to go ahead with the planned business acquisition. Only by combining these decisions can unnecessary failure be prevented (see Chapter 3).

An important part of the decision-making process is to get acceptance for the decision made, whatever the outcome. If one decides to go ahead with an acquisition, for example, getting support from both sides for the integration programme outline will be critical for an effective realization. Part of that process will consist of elaborating the outline into a full-blown integration programme as part of a joint effort.

Whether this process has to be completely top-down or not is open to discussion. We propose an approach in which the level of integration defines the decision-making structure. Certainly in those cases where new management has to be appointed, their involvement seems important. Consistency, based on the accepted vision, is certainly also important if the integration is to be effective.

INTEGRATION PROGRAMME PLAN

The development of an adequate integration programme cannot be done without a formal plan, which we call the integration programme plan. This is defined as the collection of implementation plans for all integration activities and projects which are part of the integration programme. Each plan is designed and evaluated according to the earlier defined performance criteria. Each plan needs approval before it can be implemented.

An integration programme plan will be designed in such a way that the short-term activities and projects will be much more detailed than those for the medium and long term.

The following topics need to be addressed for an integration programme plan to be successful.

INTEGRATION OBJECTIVES AND ASSUMPTIONS

An integration programme plan will contain a list of assumptions which have guided the design of the integration programme. It will also contain a clear description of the integration objectives and their interrelations.

Since an integration programme will change over time, the criteria used to decide on the selection of new activities and their prioritization will also have to be explicit.

INTEGRATION PROGRAMME STRUCTURE

The overall integration programme structure is described in this part of the integration programme plan. This includes a description of all activities, intermediate results and interfaces. The objectives–activities network presented earlier is vital here.

This part of the integration programme plan also includes the definition of the timing of all the activities and projects that are part of the integration programme. These include the start date, end date, resources allocated and the sequence of events.

It is important that all internal interfaces and linkages are made explicit, because these will have to be managed during the running of the programme. The same is true for the 'external' interfaces.

INTEGRATION PROGRAMME PROGRESS CONTROL

This section describes which progress monitoring systems will be used and how progress will be reported.

As described earlier (Chapter 4, Part I), many companies find it hard to measure integration success. Besides managing the integration by using traditional programme control variables, there should be some insight into the progress that has been made towards achieving the end results and, ultimately, the main goals.

In order to avoid a lack of clarity in integration monitoring, great attention should be paid in the planning phase to the definition of measurable objectives for each phase and each project, and to the methods that will be used to measure the integration benefits and costs. If this is done correctly, one should ideally be able to say at a specific time, 'the integration programme is over', and calculate the net result.

Balanced Integration Scorecard

It is essential for integration success that the focus within the integration goals is not exclusively on the financial benefits. To balance performance control between the hard and soft sides, the concept of a Balanced Integration Scorecard can be used to distinguish between objectives from the following perspectives: finance, customers, business processes and learning/innovation. If used correctly, it may be possible to mobilize and exploit intangible assets during integration.

Managing time and capacity

Our experience shows that many integration projects in organizational change are slowed down by a lack of time available for the necessary project activities. Very often, employees are asked to participate in projects and work together in organizational settings different from their normal positions. This causes tension with the functional manager, who has to deal with a loss of capacity.

The integration manager has to ensure that employees will not focus too much on the integration tasks and lose concentration on their normal work, which may cause performance to drop. Project leaders and integration programme management should be able to manage time and capacity by using programme management control tools. One way or another, an overall view of the available resources in a company must lead towards a realizable integration effort that sets the right priorities for both areas in a company.

INTEGRATION PROGRAMME CONTRIBUTION EVALUATION

This is designed to evaluate all of the programme results with regard to their level of contribution to the realization of the desired integration programme objectives.

INTEGRATION PROGRAMME FINANCE

Based on the planned life cycle, the required financial results (added value), agreed budgets, required financial means and planned turnover increase or cost reductions are described. This in turn can be translated into a discounted cash flow scheme for the entire project.

INTEGRATION PROGRAMME REVIEW CYCLE

This section of the integration programme plan defines in which way (procedure), how often and by whom the programme plan will be reviewed, and how *ad hoc* change requests will be dealt with.

INTEGRATION PROGRAMME ORGANIZATION

Every integration programme requires adequate organization if it is to be realized. In this section, we will look first at the list of key players in the integration organization. Furthermore, the issue of centralization of this integration organization will be discussed. Finally, the capabilities needed by the integration organization will be mentioned.

KEY PLAYERS

In each integration programme, a number of (groups of) key players can be identified, which will be briefly discussed here. Before going into this, we would like to point out a golden rule when defining the integration programme organization.

Joint teams

Based on practical experience, we are convinced that success in realizing the acceptance of the integration objectives and the commitment of the employees is a *sine qua non.* Whatever the objectives, and whatever the level of integration, no success can be achieved by designing and implementing the integration programme one-sidedly.

There is only one realistic way to set up the integration programme organization, and that is to involve representatives of all the companies or units involved. Formulated in a different way: all internal stakeholders should be part of the integration programme organization in one way or another.

So *joint* is one key word. The other is *team.* There is no way that adequate integration can take place without real cooperation in a team-like effort. Teams will vary over time and they will vary in various phases of the integration project. But teams will be the core of the integration programme organization. They will be joint teams: i.e. composed of people from the various units involved – be they companies, divisions etc. Teams will be cross-border (whether functional, process or geographical) or joint teams if they are to be effective.

Top management

Integration programmes are usually of strategic importance to the company(ies) involved, and therefore top management should largely define the integration programmes. They will decide on the key assumptions and conditions (timing, budget, resources).

They should also act as leaders to set the vision if this integration process concerns the entire company. Otherwise, this can be done by a divisional management team.

In the case of mergers, 'top management' means the new top management responsible for the newly defined company. In acquisitions 'top management' refers to those at the top of the acquiring company and the top of the acquired company.

Supervisory Board

Although it often seems to have a limited role, the Supervisory Board plays a key part in the decision process for planned business integrations. Of course, mergers will have the greatest impact, but acquisitions need approval of the Supervisory Board.

Again, depending on the business integration case, a new Supervisory Board must be set up (in the case of a merger) or a new member must be added (because of a large acquisition).

Integration programme steering group

Each integration programme should have a steering group, which is responsible for ensuring the success of the planned integration. This group should approve the integration programme, provide sufficient means and make the necessary decisions during the running of the integration programme.

M&A team

A number of large companies have a so-called Mergers & Acquisitions team, whose role is to perform all the activities necessary to acquire companies and/or prepare a merger deal. The focus in this team is on the deal, not on the actual integration. They will be phased out of the integration programme organization sooner or later. It is important, however, that the integration programme management, together with the M&A team, are involved in the deal-making phase at the earliest possible moment (see above). But it is also important that the handover between the M&A team and the integration programme management is done perfectly.

Together, the teams should evaluate the integration programme's outcomes after it is completed and use the lessons learned to upgrade the company's own Business Integration Approach.

Integration programme management

Another player is the integration programme manager, who is responsible for realizing the integration programme. Because of the impact of an integration programme, its manager will usually be a senior manager.

This role is a difficult one, and not every senior manager is qualified to fill it. Based on experience in the projects and on the discussion in Wijnen (1994), the following capabilities have been identified:

- interdisciplinary knowledge and experience in key areas of the programme
- deep knowledge about the existing organization, opinion leaders in it, understanding the unwritten rules etc.
- convincing and tenacious, but not stubborn
- committed to the integration programme, but does not represent one specific interest or party
- programme management competences and experience

This seems to be asking for the impossible. In particular, the second and fourth requirements make it almost impossible to find one person who meets all the criteria. Therefore a practical solution is to appoint at least two integration programme managers, one from each company or organizational unit involved.

Integration programme office

In a task as complex as integrating two organizations, a lot of work needs to be done. Often separate programme organizations are built to realize the task. To keep control over the whole venture it useful to set up an integration programme office (sometimes called headquarters), where communication is taken care of, employees can direct their questions and concerns to, project leaders hand in progress reports, archives are kept, meetings are held etc.

If the right attention is paid to setting up and 'dressing up' this HQ, it can function as a symbol for the integration. An integration logo that is used on any material associated with the programme helps to exploit this symbol and display the message that this is a serious business and great attention is paid to the operation.

Of course, this is a joint office consisting of people from the organizational entities involved.

Works Council

In many western European companies a Works Council exists in some form or other. As the representatives of employees – according to laws of the country (or countries) involved – it must play a particular role.

Depending on the type of integration, more than one council may be involved (for example in a merger or an acquisition). Certainly, if full integration is aimed for, joint advice from the Works Councils involved is better than having two separate and possibly contradictory outcomes. To handle these situations, a Temporary Joint Works Council could be set up, consisting of representatives of both Works Councils from the companies involved. Apart from the formal legal handling of the issues, this approach guarantees a shared view and debate about the way forward in the integration.

Again, involving the Works Council at the earliest possible moment has the big advantage of ensuring early support, and if the council opposes anything, for whatever reason, this should be taken into account in the decision-making process.

By also involving the Works Council in the integration programme organization – which can be done in various ways – a commitment and joint effort to deal with the integration programme development and realization can be achieved.

Integration programme personnel

This is another group of key players – those who will perform the activities required to realize the integration objectives. They must have certain basic skills in order to act effectively, as well as some specific skills depending on the activity that they will perform or the project they will lead or participate in (see also pp. 112–113).

One way to stimulate the acceptance of the planning and realization is to set up the integration programme together with the employees of both organizations. This is a good way of getting to know each other better. It is important to involve employees from operations because of their knowledge and experience. They should do the reality check to see whether the perceived benefits can be realized and how this can be done in the most efficient and effective way.

LEVEL OF CENTRALIZATION: CRITERIA

Wijnen (1994) has pointed out that many different forms of programme organization do exist – even within the same organization. The key is the level of centralization. By using his and our experience, the following criteria for deciding on the level of centralization have been developed.

Strategic value of the integration programme

The more important an integration programme, the more likely it is that it will be centralized. A merger realization cannot be other than a highly centralized enterprise if this is to be successful.

Value disciplines

The choice of a more centralized programme organization depends, among other things, on the chosen value discipline(s) of the companies or units to be integrated. If operational excellence is dominant, a more centralized approach will be used than in a situation in which customer intimacy is the chosen value discipline.

Size of the integration programme

The bigger the integration programme becomes – i.e. the more there is at stake – the more likely it is that there will be a centralized approach, because with size comes a need for an overview and for consistency of management.

Company capabilities

It will be easier to set up and run an integration programme successfully in a company in which many employees have project management capabilities.

INTERNAL CAPABILITIES

Realizing business integration requires specific capabilities that are not always available in a company. This applies to both sides: to the acquiring company as well as to the acquired company.

It is from these capabilities that successful integration can be achieved. Without them, many accidents will happen and the outcomes will not be the intended ones. Unfortunately, this is one of the most underestimated aspects of an integration process.

Required capabilities

The specific capabilities needed to ensure success in integration have been or will be presented in the various chapters of this book. At this point, we look specifically at the integration programme capabilities needed.

Some of the key capabilities are:

- process management
- programme management
- change management
- planning and control

Train/develop programme management skills

The skills that are necessary to pull off a major task such as integrating two organizations are different from those needed for day-to-day operations. Experience in managing complex one-off ventures increases the quality of integration management. The necessary skills can be collected from experienced employees within the company and from evaluations of previous change programmes. It is also a good idea to give those who are assigned to lead the integration programme a crash course on programme management.

Assign a crew of full-time programme employees

As described in our research findings earlier on, it is very hard to manage the time spent on the integration effort in relation to normal operations. It is advisable to install an integration organization that functions alongside normal operations. The leading functions in this integration organization are likely to be very demanding and are hard to fulfil along with a normal job. Assigning an integration manager gives a clear signal about who is responsible. It also removes some of the opportunity for politics to arise. This integration manager should be surrounded by other full-time integration team members, depending on the size and complexity of the integration.

Develop a clear understanding of responsibilities, tasks and integration functions

With the appointment of the integration programme management, it is clear who is responsible for the success of the integration. Generally, if they manage to make it a success, they will be rewarded with a good position in the future organization. In that way, integration success and personal success are aligned.

There are many different tasks that need to be done, and, as in normal operations, is it necessary to be clear about who is doing what. This can be prepared before the integration starts.

Use staff with high potential

Aligning personal success with organizational success has proved a key success factor. As will be shown in Chapter 5, integration ventures are ideal vehicles for personal development. Using those with high potential in these ventures not only increases the success rate, it also offers them challenging developmental circumstances.

CONCLUSION

This chapter has presented the day-to-day practice of managing the realization of integration. We have seen the importance of balanced planning, programme control and capable integration management. Also, best practices have been presented that increase the quality of integration planning and management. This is an important factor that contributes to the ultimate success.

The next chapter covers another important issue. Away from the 'technical' approach of managing the effort lies the challenge of successfully handling 'soft' issues. Research has shown time and time again that this is one of the most important factors in the success or failure of integration. We call our approach to this issue 'Integrational Learning'.

5

INTEGRATIONAL LEARNING: MANAGING THE 'SOFT SIDE' OF BUSINESS INTEGRATION

❖

INTRODUCTION

Earlier in this book, we referred to the rather low success rates for mergers, acquisitions and internal integration. More than half of these ventures failed – some assume that more than 70 per cent fail. This is a very serious business problem because of the value that is being destroyed, and because of the suffering and frustration experienced by those who are considered key assets in any company: its employees!

The 'soft side' of business integration

Many of the key reasons for failure are linked to the management of the so-called 'soft side' of business integration. By *soft side* we mean the aspects of business integration that in one way or another concern people and the role that they play in a business integration venture.

Into the soft category, according to our definition, fall all people-related issues. This is a very broad category because people-related aspects can be found in almost any part of business integration.

To give an impression, look at the following list of people-related issues:

- reduction of headcount
- communication
- culture
- management style
- management development

- unwritten rules
- payment packages
- right person in the right place (job)
- decision-making processes
- irrational aspects, such as 'personal chemistry'

The so-called 'hard side' of business integration refers to the financial, legal and fiscal aspects of the deal or the decision to integrate, which are usually described in a contract.

Some facts and figures

Although the percentages may vary, in most publications the following issues are mentioned as the primary reasons for failure in business integration:

- people issues: approximately 30 per cent
  not getting along with top management and culture issues (different values and norms; company and country culture)
- understanding the 'other' company's issues: approximately 25 per cent
  not understanding the specifics of the other company's way of operating
- objectives and strategy issues: approximately 15 per cent
  lack or absence of understanding of the reasons for the planned business integration and the business objectives that will have to be achieved

Soft is hard

Calling these factors 'soft' seems to be missing the point. By now it has become clear that these factors are often more important to the success of business integration than the so-called hard factors.

OVERVIEW OF THIS CHAPTER

This understanding has led us to look more carefully at this element of business integration. If the success rate of business integration ventures is to be improved, a more effective way of managing these soft issues will be needed.

Part I: Current practices

The best way to start, from our point of view, was to investigate what is really done by companies with regard to these issues. Part I therefore contains, based on our research, a description of current practices. How did the participating companies handle soft issues? We focused on three key issues:

- people
- culture
- communication

Part II: Best practices

Part II contains an overview of emerging best practices for managing these and other soft issues, based on our research with the involved companies.

Having had (much) experience with business integration, the managers that we interviewed were asked what they would do differently and what they had learned worked well in managing soft issues. So, in this part you will find what experienced managers now see as best practices in this area. These practices, because they are based on experience, are very practical and down to earth.

Part III: Framework approach

In Part III we present our framework for managing the soft side of business integration, taking into account the experiences presented in Part I and II.

We are convinced that only an integrated approach will significantly increase the success rate of business integration ventures. This framework, which is based on the best practices identified, integrates these into a consistent and holistic approach for managing the soft side using our integrational learning perspective (Figure 5.1). In this part we will clarify this integrational learning approach and outline how this helps to increase the success rate of business integration.

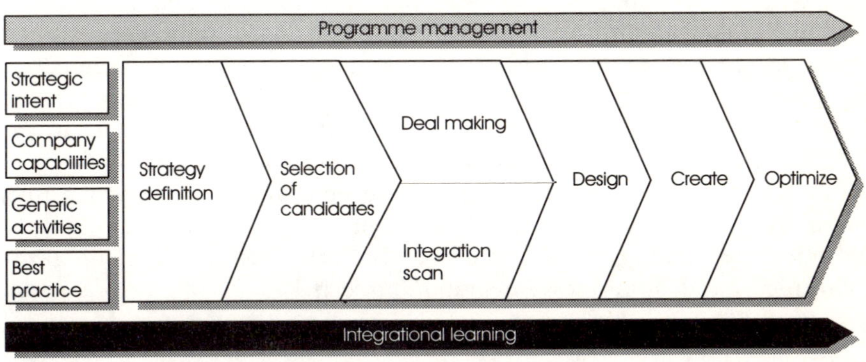

Figure 5.1 The Business Integration Approach.

PART I: CURRENT PRACTICES IN MANAGING THE SOFT SIDE

In this part an overview of current practices of how companies manage three key soft issues is presented. It describes the real-life experience of top managers.

Although many more issues can be identified, we have chosen people, culture and communication as three headings under which to group a number of practices that all relate to the management of soft-side issues. This section summarizes these practices in order to create an understanding of the practicalities of everyday business integration projects.

PEOPLE

IT IS ALL ABOUT PEOPLE

The parallels between mergers and marriages have been drawn so often that they do not need to be repeated here, except for one aspect. People are as vital to this form of business integration (and to acquisitions and internal integrations) as they are in marriage. Everything boils down to people.

This can be seen in all phases of business integration. Initially a chemistry between top managers is required to get the process started (Chapter 3). From the start irrational or emotional elements play a crucial role in the further development or break-up of the integration process. During the realization of the planned integration people still play the most important role, and therefore so do emotions and irrationality.

Under the heading of People, practices are described regarding the following aspects of business integration projects:

- staffing of critical positions
- planned outflow of employees
- retaining key employees
- motivating employees
- terms and conditions
- managing resistance to change.

Current practices for each topic will be briefly presented in the following sections.

STAFFING CRITICAL POSITIONS

The successful realization of a merger, acquisition or internal integration depends largely on the right staffing of critical positions. Most companies used a top-down appointment policy, i.e. first they appoint top management and then cascade down to the next layer.

Appointment policy

About 25 per cent of companies used a central planning mechanism (a committee or new top management) to decide on the key positions. Several companies also focused on possible 'change agents', who were appointed early in the process. As to the timing, it was noticed that only 20 per cent of the companies identified and staffed critical functions prior to closing the deal. These were all cases of full integration and mergers.

Another way to resource positions in the new organization(s) was for everybody to apply for a job, including top management. Non-executive board members formed the review committee which appointed the executive directors, who in turn acted as the appointment committee for the next layer and so on.

Duplicated functions

A number of issues around this theme have been identified. Although the level of integration will increase the problem, in almost all cases the issue of how to handle duplicated functions arose. Approximately 80 per cent of the companies saw this as a major issue. In a number of cases, where the company could offer this, internal mobility was made available.

A special case can be found in those situations where country organizations are integrated into regional ones. In these situations, equal representation of country members can become an issue. Different solutions to this problem were used, varying from neatly balancing representatives from the countries involved to completely ignoring the nationality of the candidates and focusing only on personal qualities and competencies.

Top management of the acquired company

Another issue was the handling of the top management of an acquired company. Those who selected a minimal integration scenario opted for leaving them in the driving seat, assuming that they knew the market and the company.

However, others, who chose a full or partial integration approach, showed different behaviour. One company replaced the existing top management with their 'own' managers at the start of the implementation. Several other companies also preferred this line of action, but only replaced current management when this was possible. It took some time to find the right candidates after the deal was signed.

Replacing key managers with one's 'own' people was seen as an effective measure to ensure control over the newly acquired company.

Having the right set of criteria for appointing top management during a merger is a very important topic. Most companies stated that they used a mixed set: rational or business reasons were used as well as political and personal reasons.

According to the participating managers, a merger requires a balanced representation on the new board. Knowing that reality is always more complex than the ideal, this almost always implied some sub-optimal appointments initially, because these are needed to get acceptance and alignment. In the next period these 'problem appointments' were then corrected.

PLANNED OUTFLOW OF EMPLOYEES

Many integration projects lead to changes in the number of employees. Quantitative changes in headcount are usually related to the strategic intent of the business integration as well as the level of integration. When business integration is primarily driven by cost reduction and companies or units are fully integrated, headcount is usually (significantly) reduced.

In several of the participating companies headcount was reduced; the highest percentage was 20 per cent, but in most cases the planned outflow of personnel was limited, varying from the departure of a single person to several per cent of the current personnel.

Social plan

Despite this low outflow rate, approximately 40 per cent of the companies had developed a social plan and agreed this with the Works Council and the labour unions. This indicates the careful way in which the outflow of employees was handled and how this is part of the people management practices of modern companies. In several cases the social plan contained a paragraph stating that no forced layoffs would take place. The remaining 60 per cent of the companies did not develop a social plan because, as most indicated, there was no reason to do so.

Techniques for planned outflow management

Managing the outflow was given a lot of attention, for reasons mentioned earlier. A number of techniques were used to achieve the reduction in headcount.

- One method was to call for voluntary resignations. This was helped by implementing an adequate social plan.
- Another technique used was natural outflow. The effectiveness of this technique depended of course on the demographics of the company. Early retirement options were made available in a number of companies as part of the social plan.
- Forced layoffs were used to ensure significant headcount reductions.

- About a quarter of the companies used a mobility centre. This centre performed various functions. One was to support personnel for whom no position was available inside the company in finding a new position outside.

Intra-company mobility

Another practice was to relocate employees inside the (new) organization. About half of the participating companies used this option in various ways, whereas the other half did not.

It was recognized that job rotation is essential to avoid the departure of core capabilities from the organization. A complicating issue is the autonomy of local managers. In many cases it turned out to be difficult to 'force personnel down their throat'. If replacement was seen in this light, the chances of a successful career in these new positions were not favourably evaluated.

RETAINING KEY EMPLOYEES

In all integration projects a lot of people get nervous, and a serious risk of losing key management and key personnel arises. The way in which this issue was handled varied significantly between the companies involved.

Unplanned departure of personnel did happen. For instance, in one case people left because they did not want to move to another city or country following the relocation of the company's head-office.

No action

About 40 per cent of the companies did not take specific measures to retain key employees. In one case the management perceived this as a situation about which they could do nothing.

In other companies a lot of attention was given to managing the planned outflow of staff, but not to those who should be retained. The HR capacity was dedicated to streamlining the outflow and by doing so avoiding major problems. Some managers indicated that they had not thought that it would be necessary to use retaining actions.

We could not find a relationship with the level of integration or with strategic intent.

Retaining actions

Those companies that did try to keep (talented) key employees used a range of actions. Some started to take measures before the acquisition deal was closed. Several companies made a contract with top managers, during the negotiations, to stay in an attempt to retain knowledge of market and company. This was the case in several minimal integration situations.

Most of the managers interviewed indicated that they had taken actions after the deal was done. Some of these were:

- offering new jobs with a new challenge
- offering a promotion
- offering an increase in salary
- immediate appointment to key jobs in the integration organization
- other individualized actions

This last category is rather vague, but must not be underestimated. It contains all the informal actions by management in which key staff are informed about a (planned) merger/acquisition and about their role in it as part of the attempt to retain them. Bonding with specific colleagues as well as using personal networks were also part of this last category.

All these actions were specifically mentioned in projects in which full integration was aimed for.

MOTIVATING EMPLOYEES

Apart from focusing on key personnel, a number of companies developed activities to motivate their managers and personnel. Communication was used by all (see pp. 128–132). Approximately 70 per cent performed additional motivational activities and 30 per cent did not. What were these motivational activities?

Training and support

Most of these were training activities for managers. In one merger this was used to assist the development of a shared mind-set. Stress management training was also offered. In another case, training for change management was provided. This company also offered the services of a relocation or mobility centre as well as visits to the new work environment. Another company offered counselling facilities and psychological support to its employees.

Events

Several companies organized big events like a party to celebrate the relocation part of the integration process. Others organized get-to-know-each-other events. Depending on the size of the companies involved, these events became really big projects which were seen as very important in the integration process.

Involving personnel

The majority of the companies realized that one way to motivate personnel was to involve them actively in the integration process. In these cases a link could also be identified with the level of integration: those companies aiming for full integration more often involved personnel than those aiming for partial or minimal integration.

The involvement of employees in the integration process took various forms. In several mergers department heads were made responsible for realizing the integration. In other cases, employees were part of the integration or functional teams. A more passive form of involvement was the use of personnel surveys, which were used to identify key concerns among personnel.

TERMS AND CONDITIONS

One issue that often comes up in business integration is the harmonization of labour terms and conditions (T&C), which are also called benefits and compensations.

Different answers were given, but all companies agreed that this was a complex issue that was bound to have a serious impact on both employee morale and the future performance of the company.

Although a link with the level of integration can be found – in the case of full integration it was likely that these labour terms and conditions would be synchronized – reality is more complex than that. One merged company developed completely new T&C, whereas several others tried to combine the existing T&Cs. Some made no changes at all.

In a takeover, some companies' acquirers preferred to impose their T&C, but others preferred to use the T&C of the acquired company. In several cases the economic reasons behind this decision were obvious because personnel costs would rise significantly if the T&C of the acquiring company were to be implemented, and in so doing would make the deal less attractive.

In the internal integration cases, national boundaries proved to be an important factor. Different national legal systems either did not allow or hindered complete harmonization of T&C.

In a few cases the integration process was supported by special bonus schemes that were put in place. In one case, variable pay was introduced and linked to the merger objectives and their realization, but most companies had not planned anything in this respect. Several indicated that they had rewarded several people who had been very active, but that they had done this after the integration was 'completed'.

MANAGING RESISTANCE TO CHANGE

People, when placed in uncertain situations such as an integration process, will react; part of this reaction can be to resist the realization of the integration. When asked what they had done about this, different answers were given by the participating companies.

Those companies that had elaborate change management in place had thought about managing resistance and designed measures – both proactive and reactive. However, a number of companies had not thought about it and had done nothing about it.

One approach – in a case of minimal integration – was to leave the current management in charge. They should be able to handle any negative impact related to the takeover. One company said that it tried to create a relationship based on confidence and trust by not forcing corporate rules onto the acquired company. This, of course, does not work for partial or full integration.

In most cases communication at the outset of the integration process as well as during the whole integration was seen to play an important role in handling resistance.

CULTURE

CULTURE IS EVERYWHERE

For those who have worked abroad, it will not be difficult to recognize culture differences. However, almost the same multitude of cultural differences exists within the boundaries of a single nation as well. Companies do differ in their cultures, and these differences seriously affect performance, as Collins and Porras (1994) have shown. The intangible nature of culture and its serious affect on performance make this a major topic for business integration.

Culture and its impact were discussed in every interview. Culture was (often looking back) seen as (very) important, especially when management recognized afterwards that serious differences in culture existed.

In this section the following aspects will be presented:

- culture assessment
- company culture
- company and country culture

CULTURE ASSESSMENT

One of our questions was whether or not a culture assessment of the entities involved had been performed as part of the decision-making process and as part of preparing the integration plan. It turned out that more than 60 per cent of the companies had not performed a culture assessment (see Table 5.1)! No link with the level of integration could be established.

Table 5.1 Culture assessment utilization.

Culture assessment (*n*)	Merger	Acquisition	Internal integration
Yes	1	3	2
No	4	4	1

The need for a culture assessment was, in a number of cases, seen as not very important, because a company within the same country was taken over or was merged with and it was assumed that no cultural differences would exist.

Those companies that did assess culture used various methods. A few companies performed an assessment as part of the due diligence process in the buying phase. This was done in one case using employees of the acquiring company. In another case a culture assessment model was used to assess the differences. In a third case a survey among employees was used to identify cultural differences.

In another case (merger), management decided not to do an initial cultural assessment. However, once the integration process was under way they revised their decision and organized one. A randomly selected number of employees from both companies were invited to small group meetings in which culture issues were identified and discussed. In doing so they came across a number of important differences:

- *Differences in basic values*: one company was more pragmatic in its operation whereas the other operated from a more normative view; another difference concerned internal openness.
- *Differences in orientation*: one company used a process orientation, whereas the other was results-oriented.
- *Differences in relation to the outside world*: a privately owned company versus a public company.

This approach also demonstrated that a large number of similarities existed as well. These could be found in the level of change in both companies, a high level of service orientation towards customers, a high degree of loyalty among employees and a willingness to change.

CULTURAL INTEGRATION: COMPANY CULTURE OR CULTURES?

Nowadays, most managers would say that effective integration management can only take place if cultural differences and similarities have been assessed and linked to the strategic intent.

The managers interviewed recognized that often the assumption of similar cultures turned out to be either false or at least an oversimplification. It took time to discover cultural differences; often these were discovered as an

Table 5.2 Overview of current practices regarding cultural integration.

	Full integration	Partial integration	Minimal integration
Required culture	❍ Two separate cultures ❍ One new culture ❍ (Equal) mix of both cultures ❍ One dominant culture	❍ Separate cultures ❍ Acquirer forced its culture ❍ Mix of both cultures	❍ Separate cultures (cultures match)

underlying factor when integration problems were analysed. Furthermore, to manage cultural differences it was seen as essential to have a clear understanding about the desired culture for the new entity as well as about the existing cultures.

The companies involved provided examples of different ways of handling cultural issues. Most companies said that they had tried to influence the cultural differences, although this meant different things for different companies.

We encountered different 'solutions' to the problem of what to do with the culture of the companies involved in a business integration venture. In Table 5.2 we have summarized the various 'solutions' we found in relation to the level of integration that was aimed for.

In trying to answer the question of what the culture for the 'new' entity after the integration should be, companies varied significantly when trying to get to a single culture, either by designing a 'new' culture or by forcing one culture onto the other entity. We also came across cases where no cultural integration took place.

Full integration

In those cases in which full integration was the objective, many variations in handling cultural components could be found. For instance, the coexistence of two cultures, a mixed (new) culture and one culture that became dominant were found.

The last occurred in a merger in which significant cultural differences were identified at the beginning of the integration process. These concerned basic values, management style and systems, customer management etc. Top management decided to point out what they thought was important and to let the changes happen from there, and it chose the culture of one of the two merging parties. This led to a lot of struggle, but in the end this seems to have been accepted in the new company.

Partial integration

In cases where partial integration was aimed for, various ways of handling cultural integration were found. In one case, the cultural fit was limited.

Serious differences existed between the acquiring and acquired companies. These differences were found in customer orientation; the methods of decision making; and the use of a consensus-focused approach vs. a results-oriented approach. A conscious process, consisting mainly of communication efforts, has subsequently led to a workable mix of the two previous cultures.

In another case major cultural differences existed between two companies, one of which was taken over by the other. These differences regarded basic values such as the meaning of work (must primarily be fun etc.) as well as management style (formal, hierarchical vs. informal), management systems (control and results-driven vs. hierarchical escalation) etc. However, no specific actions for cultural integration were taken.

In yet another case, serious differences between the acquirer's culture and that of the acquired company were found. The acquiring company saw its culture as the dominant one and assumed that this was to be absorbed by the acquired company. This approach was used in a quarter of all researched cases.

Minimal integration

As can be seen in Table 5.2 there was a certain logic in minimal integration cases. Maintaining separate cultures was here seen as practical, especially in those cases where a cultural assessment in the deal phase had ensured that a certain basic match of culture did exist. This facilitated sufficient communication, working together and exchanging experience and expertise, without the need to further integrate the (local) cultures.

COMPANY AND COUNTRY CULTURE

Most of the mergers, acquisitions and internal integrations that were studied in this project took place inside the borders of one country. In only a few cases was cross-border integration aimed for. In these latter cases country culture and language turned out to be very important factors that had to be taken into account if one was to succeed in integrating two or more separate entities.

The presence of a strong company culture was seen as a supporting factor, but this was not enough to straighten out the local cultural differences. Even a number of years after the integration process had been completed, differences still existed and needed careful managing in one company. It was also recognized that in some parts of the new company country culture played a dominant role and was given an opportunity to do so.

In those cases where a new culture was defined, management initiated measures to ensure that this culture could be realized. Realizing this change from the existing culture to the newly defined culture turns out to be a very time-consuming and complex process. In several mergers employees from different companies were located in the same building to assist the cultural integration process.

COMMUNICATION

COMMUNICATION, COMMUNICATION AND... COMMUNICATION

As in any change process, communication plays a key role, said all participating companies. And yet almost all of them concluded in the end that they had not done enough of it.

This section presents practices concerning the following aspects of communication:

- communication objectives
- communication plan
- communication to stakeholders
- communication media

COMMUNICATION OBJECTIVES AND PLAN

Objectives

In the business integration projects that we looked at, different objectives were mentioned for communication activities. The main objective mentioned, however – whatever the media of communication – was to inform stakeholders about the (intended) business integration. A second objective that was mentioned was to get employees committed to the planned integration. A third objective was to position the new company – in the case of a merger – in the market.

Communication plan

Most companies planned their communication to stakeholders and drew up a communication plan. These plans identified stakeholders and the media that were used to communicate with them. The need for a communication plan was recognized by all the companies involved.

Although this is more difficult to plan, informal communication was seen as very important in business integration processes. Some companies underlined the need to plan informal communication opportunities, but most of the planned communication activities had a formal character.

COMMUNICATION TO STAKEHOLDERS

Communication regarding business integration was aimed at individuals, groups or entities that had a stake in the company. We call stakeholders who are part of the company internal stakeholders. Table 5.3 lists the stakeholders that were mentioned. Those we have defined as external stakeholders can be found outside the company.

Table 5.3 Overview of stakeholders.

External stakeholders	Internal stakeholders
Government	Supervisory Board
Monopoly authorities	Management
Customers	Personnel
Suppliers	Works Council
Shareholders	Unions
News media	Relatives of personnel

Communication in the case of a merger or takeover usually starts with national or regional authorities, which either must be informed or must approve the planned merger or takeover. The press and customers are usually informed once the deal is done. At the same time internal stakeholders are informed.

COMMUNICATION MEDIA

A large number of communication media were used. An overview is presented in Table 5.4.

Table 5.4 Overview of communication media.

Media for external communication	Media for internal communication
Meetings	
Client visit	Personnel meeting Regular communication inside departments Visits of the CEO/Board to all sites (roadshow) Visit the other company 'Corridor' meetings
Written	
Press release Letter to clients Letter to supplier Article or CEO interview	Integration bulletin/newsletter Company magazine Company brochures Letter to the personnel Bulletin boards Posters Booklet with answers to often asked questions
Electronic	
Client telephone call	Company TV Email Intranet
Other	
	Central question coordination

External communication media

Clients were often mentioned as the key stakeholders with whom communication was of the greatest importance. The media chosen varied from personal visits by the CEO or a Board member (in the case of a key client) or by an account manager to a personal call from a top manager or a (standard) letter in which they were informed about the (planned) integration and the impact on the relationship with the client.

Of course, most business integrations were communicated via the press at an early stage, when, for instance, the deal was made. Often clients received a letter in which they were informed about the motives for the planned or realized merger or internal integration. This usually included an explanation about what was to change for them (either nothing or new benefits for clients, depending on the intent of the integration).

Of course, in a number of cases the press asked to interview one or more key players in (for example) a merger, which led to dedicated articles in various newspapers or other written media.

Internal communication media

The intensity of internal communication is influenced significantly by the level of integration. In those cases where full integration was aimed for, internal communication was most intense and many media were used. The opposite was true in those cases where minimal integration was the objective.

Meetings

Because of the nature and impact of business integration, personal contact between top management and personnel is considered to be a necessity – certainly in the cases of full and partial integration.

Special integration meetings were organized to inform personnel about the logic of the integration. Often in those meetings new management were presented to the staff. In order to inform personnel at various sites, top management visited those sites to bring the 'gospel' and get personnel committed to the planned integration. This happened in only a few cases.

Another interesting meeting was a visit of the employees from the company that was taken over to a site of the company that now owned them. By visiting a site and meeting their future colleagues, the process of getting acquainted could be started.

Very often communication about integration was done through regular company department meetings. In these, information was cascaded down the company via line management. This was less time-consuming. The downside of this type of communication was seen as the way in which information changed from level to level in the company(ies) involved.

Naturally, a lot of informal meetings took place in corridors and elsewhere. The importance of these meetings should not be underestimated, although it is difficult to manage them. Several companies said that they had used a lot of informal meetings in the beginning to commit key personnel and inform them about the progress of the deal.

Written media

Most companies used written media more often than any other. A letter to all the personnel involved was among the most often used media, as were articles in the company magazine. These were used to explain the integration logic and present the outline of the planned integration. They usually said something about the key managers in the new situation. When a new house style was implemented this was also published.

Often a dedicated integration magazine or newsletter was published during the entire integration process, containing information about the progress of the integration project. Where full integration was to be achieved, these magazines were used to inform staff about the plans, new visions, new images, progress etc. Descriptions of the business integration organization were also part of the content presented. In other cases, pictures of the new office building were added to give employees an impression of the new working environment. Dealing with all sorts of questions in a 'frequently asked questions' section also proved to be informative.

In a few cases all the employees received company brochures at their home address so that families could learn a bit more about the company that had taken over the company where their relative worked.

Bulletin boards were used which contained progress reports and other relevant information. Posters were put up to inform personnel about new mission statements, company logos etc.

One company supplied its staff with a small booklet in which the answers to frequently asked questions were presented. In this case, the questions concerned issues related to the relocation of the company and the compensation measures.

Other

In one case the company organized a central database of questions that had been asked as well as the answers that had been given in order to make sure that the same answers were given to the same questions throughout the company.

QUALITY OF COMMUNICATION

Many participants stressed the importance of honest and direct communication, and identified that it was difficult to communicate sufficiently. They recognized that there is a big risk in waiting too long to communicate with employees about a planned business integration. Although the desire to wait until 'everything' is clear was seen as understandable, this was not seen as an effective way of communicating internally. The importance of communicating more often was stressed.

Finally, as is well understood, communication is a two-way process in which a lot of things can go wrong. Only a few companies tried to establish whether the receivers of the communications had understood the message. Most companies, despite their communication plans, did not do so.

CURRENT PRACTICES

The practices presented in the preceding sections do not cover all soft issues; on the contrary, they concern only the three main topics: people, culture and communication. With these, we hope to have demonstrated the variety of existing practices as well as the ways in which many companies have tried to deal with the issues. Reading between the lines, you probably noticed that they did not always do this very effectively. Therefore we move on to Part II, where we present what was learned and what the companies now consider best practices.

PART II: BEST PRACTICES IN MANAGING THE SOFT SIDE OF BUSINESS INTEGRATION

INTRODUCTION

Many companies now have some or a lot of experience with business integration. Although many of the current practices in the soft side of business integration seem to be frustrating, a lot has been learned about managing the soft side of these ventures by those who have tried to realize integration projects.

Using the methodology described in the introduction, experienced top managers have identified what they now consider best practices for managing the soft side of business integration. In this part, we present their views and share what has been the result of hard work, a lot of frustration, experimentation and sometimes luck.

In discussing the designated best practices, we decided to split them into various categories. One group of best practices was seen by the participating managers as applicable to all business integration projects. These we have called generic best practices and are presented on pp. 133–137. Generic best practices all contribute to the realization by management of the soft side of business integration.

The second group of best practices are those whose effectiveness varies depending on the level of integration aimed for. This group we have called specific best practices. We present these best practices on pp. 137–148 and also relate them to the previously defined three levels of integration (see Chapter 3).

GENERIC BEST PRACTICES

Generic best practices are those that, according to the managers involved, apply to all business integration projects, independent of the strategic intent or the level of integration.

In this section, a brief description of each generic best practice will be presented. Each practice has been rated by the participating managers from the perspective of how much this contributes to the successful management of the soft side of business integration ventures. They used a rating scale which varied from very low (1) to very high (5). Table 5.5 presents an overview of the generic best practices identified and their scores as given by the participants in the study. Most of the scores are high and show a high degree of agreement as to the level of contribution of each of the best practices. Only

Table 5.5 Generic best practices.

	Generic practice	Average score
1	Top management appointment	4.8
2	Communication plan	4.5
3	Joint integration teams	4.4
4	Top management explanation	4.3
5	Focus on remaining personnel	4.2
6	Check message reception	4.2
7	Develop management development programme	4.1
8	Communicate change early	4.0
9	Joint presentations	3.8
10	Organizational and personal development	3.7

Scale: 1 = very low contribution; 5 = very high contribution

with regard to those in places 9 and 10 did some participants indicate that they estimate the contribution to be relatively low.

We now present a brief description of each of these best practices.

1. TOP MANAGEMENT APPOINTMENT

At the top of the list, the managers placed the appointment of top management as soon as possible to ensure that this group stays committed. Appointment can mean reconfirming their position as the top management of a company that was taken over. It can also mean the appointment of new management to become the top team.

They should be made directly responsible in order to avoid a period in which a responsibility vacuum exists. Top management should start their work as quickly as possible to ensure that the integration process will take place.

Best practice is to appoint top management as early as possible. If feasible, they should be involved in the strategic decision-making process from the beginning.

2. COMMUNICATION PLAN

Second on the list of generic practices was the development of a communication plan. It is critical to have a well-defined plan which states not only the communication objectives but also to whom they will be communicated, which media will be used and when these communications will take place.

In such a plan communication with both external and internal stakeholders should be planned. The importance of honest and frequent communication is again underlined.

Designing a comprehensive communication plan as soon as possible and executing it consistently are deemed to be of the highest importance. As many media as possible should be used in order to communicate in many different ways and by doing so contact and commit as many stakeholders as possible.

3. JOINT INTEGRATION TEAMS

Integration always implies the getting-together in one way or another of two or more organizational entities.

In order to achieve successful integration it is deemed necessary to facilitate that process by using mixed teams that consist of representatives of all the entities involved. Although this seems the logical approach for full integration cases, it is also needed in all other situations.

Involving joint or mixed teams from the companies or units involved as soon as this is feasible is seen as contributing to managing the soft side of business integration. By doing so, integration has already started in the Design phase. This also facilitates the early discovery of possible issues that might play a role in the implementation phases. These teams are practising grounds for working together, which can provide invaluable information for the later stages of the planned business integration.

These teams should preferably be led by those who will play an important role in the new organization. Parts of the teams that perform the design work should also be involved in the implementation to ensure consistency and continuity.

4. TOP MANAGEMENT EXPLANATION

It has been repeatedly stated that integration processes always result in feelings of uncertainty about the future of the company involved and also about the future of personnel involved. Therefore it is seen as necessary that those who decide about the merger, acquisition or internal integration should take the trouble to meet all the personnel to explain the whys and hows of this process.

Top management must present an explanation for the direction-setting they have done when they decided on this business integration project and discuss this with as many stakeholders as possible to support the committing process. Their presence also allows employees to get a 'feel' for the leadership of the new company and by doing so allows them to build their personal bond with the new company (see also Part III of this chapter).

5. FOCUS ON REMAINING PERSONNEL

As was concluded in Part I of this chapter, a lot of attention is often given to those who leave the company(ies) during business integration processes.

Successful realization of the integration objectives, however, depends on those who remain with the new entity. Therefore it is very important to ensure that these employees will get enough attention to ensure that they are committed to realizing the integration objectives and that they are capable of doing everything that is necessary to do so.

Management attention should be focused on the remaining employees and not just on those who will leave the company as a result of the integration project.

6. CHECK MESSAGE RECEPTION

Looking back on the current experiences, it has been concluded that too often management assumes that the integration message has been understood. This then turns into a problem because personnel inside the company start acting on an incomplete or incorrect understanding of the integration objectives and process, leading to undesired outcomes.

It is considered important to review the reception of the integration message by key audiences to ensure that the messages are well understood and that employees can use these in defining their own actions.

This sometimes unnecessary and time-consuming effort helps to ensure that early in the process, disbelief, misunderstandings and wrong perceptions are tracked and can be dealt with effectively before they start to upset the entire implementation process.

7. DEVELOP A MANAGEMENT DEVELOPMENT PROGRAMME

Many companies have a management development programme in place to ensure that their need for qualified managers can be met using new or current staff. Changing circumstances in highly volatile markets often lead to different requirements for managers.

Business integration processes are situations which offer those with high potential a perfect opportunity to rapidly develop their management skills and attitude.

To use the opportunity of an integration project to set up a dedicated management development programme is a wise decision which offers managers many challenges from which they can gain new experiences which can be critical in managing the new integrated company.

8. COMMUNICATE CHANGE EARLY

There are never enough communication opportunities provided in integration processes. The timing of the communication is part of an open and honest communication approach.

It is considered best practice to inform employees at an early stage – including the uncertainties that go with that – about the planned business integration, in so doing ensuring trust among those involved in the integration. This should be done by also making clear what the expected roles of the employees are in the future developments.

9. JOINT PRESENTATIONS

In all situations in which two or more entities are integrated, it is deemed important to present visions in mixed or joint meetings of representatives from all entities involved.

In addition, plans for the future should be discussed in joint groups to ensure that the entities involved get the same information at the same time and share the same views about the future. By discussing these visions and plans in joint groups all sides will learn from each other by listening to their questions, worries, comments etc. Careful monitoring of these processes is required to ensure effective use of joint presentations.

10. ORGANIZATIONAL AND PERSONAL DEVELOPMENT

Every integration situation implies change at the level of the company. Sometimes the amount of change is limited (minimal integration) and sometimes everything changes (merger).

What is often overlooked is that a company consists of people, and that when companies change, people will have to change if the whole operation is to be successful. It is considered best practice to link organizational development with personal development. In Part III, we will look into this critical issue in more depth.

With this last best practice, we conclude the description of the ten generic best practices. These were seen to contribute, to a greater or lesser extent, to the improvement of the management of the soft side of any business integration project.

SPECIFIC BEST PRACTICES AND THE LEVEL OF BUSINESS INTEGRATION

Besides the generic best practices, an additional 23 best practices were identified by the participating managers. We present these best practices here. It is good to remember that experienced integration managers or top managers responsible for business integration defined these and that they are not simply the work of a consultant who had a good idea! We have presented them in the wording used by the participants in order to stay as close to their experiences as possible.

They are called specific best practices because their contributions vary, according to the participating managers, depending on the level of integration that is aimed for. Therefore they scored each practice for its contribution to the management of the soft side of business integration according to the three levels of integration: full, partial and minimal.

Because the contribution of each best practice varies with the level of integration, we have first chosen to present an initial description of each practice. This is done in alphabetical order in order to present them in a neutral fashion. Although a number of these specific best practices could be linked, we have stuck to the alphabetical order of presentation.

After that, we will look at the relationship with the level of integration. On pp. 144–145 we present an overview of the ratings that each of these practices were given for cases of full integration. In the next section, we look at partial integration and the effectiveness of these practices for managing the soft side of business integration. Finally, we deal with minimal integration on pp. 147 and 148.

DESCRIPTION OF SPECIFIC BEST PRACTICES

Appointment policy

Sometimes integration processes start off as a rather *ad hoc* type of activity, for example in those cases where an opportunity came along and top management simply decided to go for it. When the deal comes through, all of a sudden the question arises of who will manage the acquired company (for example). Who will then be appointed (or why the current management will be left in place) is often unclear, causing uncertainty and possibly frustration among key managers.

An appointment policy should be defined early on in the process and should be communicated to all involved so that a feeling of 'backroom dealings' can be avoided. This policy should, of course, include a clear procedure for the implementation, including a well-defined time frame so that all involved are aware of the various steps and when they will be completed. This will help employees to plan their personal moves accordingly and ensure sufficient speed during this part of the integration process.

Bonus

A number of incentives exist to assist people in developing the required behaviour during the integration processes. One of these is to use a bonus system. This implies that getting a bonus is directly linked to achieving clearly defined integration objectives.

It is important to ensure that existing reward systems support the integration objectives, which unfortunately will very often not be the case because current reward systems were designed for other circumstances.

Without going so far as to define the need to always design and implement an integration objectives-related bonus system, careful consideration must be given to avoid a counter-integration effect from current reward systems in one or more of the companies involved in the business integration venture.

Change education

Integration processes are certainly dependent on the high impact of human qualities. These processes are often very complex and bound to go wrong somewhere, particularly if they are not well understood.

In many companies, the level of expertise regarding change and managing change processes – especially with regard to integration management – is not very high. Therefore it seems wise to train key employees in change management and its aspects. This can be training in project management, team management, leadership or stress management.

Company brochures

The families of those who work at the company(ies) involved in the integration process are not often seen as stakeholders, yet they are the people that hear all the stories and often live on the pay packet that is brought home. For them, a lot can change because of an integration process.

It is considered best practice to inform them about the planned changes in the company or the new company for which their family member or partner will work. Sending several brochures about the history, current organization and future plans, including the new integrated part, will tell the families about the new environment for their loved ones.

Feedback workshops

Top management, as well as integration management, should know about the progress and perceptions of progress inside the company(ies) involved.

It is considered best practice to organize feedback workshops with representatives from across the organization(s) involved. In these sessions employees can express their views on progress, issues, problems and ways forward. This will help to bring out problems, issues and dissatisfaction in a controlled way and help to deal with these before major problems arise. It also helps to correct the bias with which each top manager has to do his or her job.

Informal meetings

It is widely recognized that employees of integrating entities need to understand the whys and hows. But – and this is seen as best practice – on top of that they also need to be able to meet their new colleagues in a non-work situation before they actually start to work together. A number of these meetings can be identified; they all share the same quality that they facilitate informal getting-acquainted meetings.

Integrated labour terms and conditions

Employees tend to be influenced up to a certain level by the terms and conditions of the contract that they have with the company they work for. In order to stimulate integration it is seen as important to make sure that the labour terms and conditions are the same for all personnel. This implies deciding which terms and conditions will apply and how fast these new terms and conditions can be implemented using the proper procedures.

Dealing with terms and conditions issues will also help to avoid dissatisfaction and feelings of envy. It is considered important to evaluate the terms and conditions carefully and decide whether or not to integrate these, based on a clear understanding of the full impact of every option.

Integration magazine

In order to underline the importance of an integration project, dedicated communication is required. It is seen as best practice to publish, throughout the entire project, a dedicated integrated magazine that informs all personnel about the plans and their realization. By doing so every employee will get the same information and the chances of false rumours will be reduced.

Job rotation

Uncertainty about job security in periods of integration can result in the outflow of key employees. Furthermore, effective integration often implies that the capabilities of one (part of the) company are transferred to another (part of the) company.

It is considered best practice to introduce a clear job rotation policy to ensure that key capabilities can be kept inside the company and that people are given a further development opportunity.

Me issues first

Internal communication should be clear about the integration objectives (see generic best practices) and how the process will proceed. But information should not be limited to company level only.

Communication needs to address as soon as possible the so-called 'me issues'. These are issues such as: is there a role for me in the new situation? If so, what will it be? If not, what does that mean? Who will become my colleagues? Who will be my new boss? And so on.

If these issues are not dealt with in an early phase of the integration process, employees might not accept other relevant information because they are worried too much about their personal well-being. Of course, this can and will create a lot of negative energy, which will hinder the integration and will make a lot of people unnecessarily uncomfortable. This last situation can be avoided up to a certain level by addressing these issues early in the process.

It is considered best practice to inform employees as soon as possible about the personal consequences of the planned integration project in an honest and open way.

New ways of working

Although this does not always happen, integration processes often require changes in the operating model of the entities involved. These changes, for example in processes or the IT systems used, lead to new requirements for employee behaviour. On top of that, the planned synergies often require employees to work together with new colleagues in a new working environment.

It is therefore seen as best practice to train people in these new ways of working to ensure that they not only know but also understand what is required of them and that they are capable of delivering the required behaviour. Using simulations is one way of practising new ways of working before actually entering into the new working situation.

These simulations help significantly in understanding the complexities of the new working situation as well as the pitfalls that might be part of it. Employees are also given an opportunity to experience some of the emotions attached to the new ways of working before they really start working in that environment. This also gives them the opportunity to make mistakes and experiment with new behaviour without the attached risk of the day-to-day working environment. Practising new behaviour in a simulated environment with qualified guidance from one or more trainers allows employees to learn effectively about the new situation and practice effective behaviour at the same time.

Personnel survey

Understanding employees' reactions to the planned integration is often on the mind of top management at the beginning of the adventure. But soon after the deal has been done and the actual integration process starts, this gets less and less priority. It is forgotten until something happens that rocks the boat, causing serious problems to arise.

It is seen as best practice to perform regular personnel surveys to measure employee satisfaction. These surveys should include dedicated sections about the integration process and outcomes as well as about the personal experiences of employees.

Progress communication

Communication is often intense at the beginning of an integration process. The announcement of the deal, the final agreement and the kick-off of the process are all well-known communication moments. But after that communication must go on.

Managing the soft side of business integration is supported by regularly informing all employees about the progress of the integration project using different media. Integration newsletters, bulletin boards, email, videos and, of course, informal contacts are all deemed to be very important to keep personnel informed about the progress being made and the issues that surface.

Random personnel meetings

How much do you need to know about what people in the company(ies) think about the cultural issues? It helps to invite random employees to discuss the current and new cultures to ensure that developments in this area are well understood by employees. These group meetings can be mixed in order to ascertain where the integration process stands from various points of view.

Relocation office (also called the Mobility centre or information centre)

Despite all the forms of communication, a number of employees might feel frightened to ask certain questions in a group or a public situation. In order to ensure that these people can and will ask these questions that are bothering them, it helps to set up a relocation office or information office. This office will help every individual with the questions or issues that they have regarding their future inside or outside the company. This can be done in one-to-one confidential sessions by HR specialists or outside consultants, for example, who are independent and will not pass on the information asked for by employees.

By doing so, more controlled handling can take place which reduces unnecessary unrest and uncertainty. At the same time, more effective management of the outflow and through-flow of personnel becomes possible.

Road show

Making the organizational entities involved understand the whys and hows of an integration process is very important. It is seen as best practice when top management goes on the road and visits the employees involved at their site to explain the business and integration vision and the planned implementation. This road show should help to restore or maintain confidence in top management and in so doing reduce the anxiety levels caused by the planned integration.

Salary increase

There are many incentives for employees. In difficult times – e.g. integration processes – additional incentives can help to commit people and reward them. It might help to commit employees to the company by increasing the basic salary of those people that play an important role in an integration process.

Spontaneous meetings

How much can you plan? A lot, obviously, but certainly not everything, especially where people and their emotions are concerned. Therefore it also helps to allow people certain space for spontaneous meetings and get-togethers. This will help mutual understanding to grow and by doing so help cement the integration process. How should you go about doing this? By creating opportunities that might be used. Whether these will be used or not is difficult to assess in advance.

Talented personnel

In a going concern, where all management positions are occupied, it is often difficult to create chances for talented personnel. An integration process is a superb opportunity to give talented staff members responsibility for part of this process. This gives them an opportunity to prove themselves in a challenging situation. It also gives the company the chance to bring in some 'fresh blood', which is often required in a changed environment.

Team building

Expecting people to work together is often part of integration activities. How they should do that is not always clear.

Another best practice is to organize activities that help groups of people to become a team. In this way, more realistic expectations can be defined in this area. As has already been explained, making the earliest possible start with team building helps enormously. This is also a learning opportunity in which small-scale experiments can help to understand the larger process of integration that is to take place in the creation phase (see also Chapter 2).

Team spirit

In integration processes working together becomes even more important than in a going concern. So far a lot has been said about teamwork and its impact, but ensuring that teamwork can take place requires dedicated decisions and measures.

One further best practice is to ensure that team spirit comes about by facilitating this in certain ways of working, offering team-based tools and team-based labour terms and conditions.

Top management focus

In every company top management plays an important role, and in times of change and uncertainty their role becomes even more important. Therefore it is seen as best practice to pay a lot of attention to top management to ensure that they are happy. This is based on the assumption that if they are happy they will share this with the rest of the company and by doing so help the company to perform well.

Unwritten rules communication

If one is to work successfully in a new company, one must understand what Peter Scott-Morgan (1995) so rightly called the 'Unwritten rules of the game'.

Although this may vary according to the situation, understanding these rules is needed for survival. Being able to cope with these rules is necessary if one wants to change them to align with new strategic objectives and a 'new' culture. Therefore another best practice is to make these unwritten rules explicit and communicate them to new personnel. This can be done via a presentation on the dos and don'ts in this company; on the procedures used; and on the expectations that exist regarding personal behaviour.

It always means that people will have to give up part of their current behaviour and mind-set, which takes time and can only be done effectively if it is done in a careful and understanding way.

BEST PRACTICES FOR FULL INTEGRATION

We start with an assessment of the contribution of these 23 specific practices to cases in which full integration was aimed for (Table 5.6). This form of business integration is very complex (see Chapter 3). Many of the best practices identified were seen to be contributing significantly towards the realization of the full integration objectives.

Significant agreement existed between the participating managers about those practices that were rated as contributing high and above. Most of these eight practices concern the way in which the integration process is organized and how employees are involved.

Best practices that were assessed as having an average to high contribution addressed other issues as well. A growing spread in the scores among the participants was seen. Whereas some considered top management focus to be highly important, others took the opposite view and regarded this as contributing very little.

The same differences in view can be found with setting up a relocation office. Training employees in change management was seen as highly significant by some, but others saw this as only mildly effective (score 2). Publishing an integration magazine produced even more diverse scores ranging from 1 to 4.

Table 5.6 Full integration.

Rank	Best practice for full integration	Score
High to very high contribution		
1	Integrated labour terms and conditions	4.6
2	Me issues first	4.6
3	Progress communication	4.6
4	Job rotation	4.3
5	Spontaneous meetings	4.3
6	Informal meetings	4.1
7	Unwritten rules	4.1
Average to high contribution		
8	Personnel survey	3.8
9	Company brochure	3.8
10	Appointment policy	3.7
11	Team spirit	3.7
12	Feedback workshops	3.7
13	Team building	3.7
14	Talented personnel	3.6
15	Relocation office	3.6
16	Road show	3.6
17	Integration magazine	3.3
18	Top management focus	3.3
19	Random personal meetings	3.2
20	Change education	3.1
21	Bonus	3.0
Low to average contribution		
22	New ways of working	2.7
Very low to low contribution		
23	Salary increase	1.7

The practice that caused most difference in opinion was the use of a bonus system. Whereas some saw this as having very little contribution (score: 1), others viewed this as very important (score: 5).

Rating the training of employees in new ways of working also led to differing results and a low score. The range varied from 1 to 5, but on average this practice came out rather low, which is surprising when one considers its importance in realizing full integration in everyday reality.

There was definite agreement with regard to the very limited impact of salary increases.

BEST PRACTICES FOR PARTIAL INTEGRATION

The next level is the one aiming for partial integration (see also Chapter 3). The participants rated all 23 specific practices for this model and came up with the results presented in Table 5.7.

Of the defined best practices, only four were seen as having a big impact on this type of integration. But if the top 15 are compared with those for full integration, not many differences can be identified apart from the lower scores. In this case integrating the labour terms and conditions was given a lower rating, which is linked to the issue of which parts of the operating model are being integrated and the cost issue discussed earlier (Part I).

Table 5.7 Partial integration.

Rank	Best practice for partial integration	Score
High to very high contribution		
1	Me issues first	4.4
2	Progress communication	4.0
3	Spontaneous meetings	4.0
Average to high contribution		
4	Job rotation	3.9
5	Unwritten rules	3.7
6	Company brochures	3.7
7	Appointment policy	3.6
8	Informal meetings	3.6
9	Talented personnel	3.4
10	Team spirit	3.4
11	Personnel survey	3.3
12	Integrated labour terms and conditions	3.3
13	Road show	3.3
14	Feedback workshops	3.3
15	Team building	3.3
16	Top management focus	3.1
17	Relocation office	3.0
18	Change education	3.0
19	Integration magazine	3.0
Low to average contribution		
20	Bonus	2.9
21	Random personnel meetings	2.7
22	New ways of working	2.6
Very low to low contribution		
23	Salary increase	1.7

Of the best practices presented, views on the last seven differed significantly. Focusing on top management was seen by half as effective whereas others did not think this contributed much to realizing the integration objectives.

The same is true for the use of a relocation office, a bonus system and meetings with randomly selected employees. Also, training employees in new ways of working together was rated differently ranging from 1 to 4.

Again, most managers agreed that salary increases did not really help in achieving the integration objectives.

BEST PRACTICES FOR MINIMAL INTEGRATION

As was presented in Chapter 3, minimal integration usually implies a limited exercise. Of the best practices identified, only one – spontaneous meetings – was seen as having a high impact (Table 5.8).

About ten other practices were also seen to contribute significantly, but the remaining best practices were apparently considered not to contribute much to the realization of this type of integration.

The top five practices differed significantly from those listed for full and partial integration, reflecting the different characteristics of this form of integration.

USING BEST PRACTICES IN MANAGING THE SOFT SIDE

The best practices presented in this part are based on the day-to-day integration experiences of the participating managers. They have helped to put together a better understanding of what managing the soft side of integration means and how it is best done.

The difference between generic and specific best practices is considered valuable because it helps to understand that there is a minimal level of 'professional' handling of managing the soft side business integration projects, i.e. the generic best practices. Yet at the same time it turns out to be necessary to differentiate various realities in integration projects, depending on the level of integration. The differentiations that the managers made between the various levels of integration were more mixed than might be expected.

However, as soon as you look more carefully at the complexity of each integration venture, it is easy to recognize our earlier message that each business integration project is unique. The managers involved confirmed this by pointing out that some best practices worked in one case, but not in others.

Table 5.8 Minimal integration.

Rank	Best practice for minimal integration	Score
High to very high contribution		
1	Spontaneous meetings	4.0
Average to high contribution		
2	Progress communication	3.7
3	Unwritten rules	3.4
4	Company brochures	3.3
5	Me issues first	3.3
6	Job rotation	3.3
7	Personnel survey	3.2
8	Informal meetings	3.0
9	Team spirit	3.0
Low to average contribution		
10	Road show	2.7
11	Feedback workshops	2.7
12	Team building	2.7
13	Top management focus	2.7
14	Talented personnel	2.4
15	Appointment policy	2.1
16	Change education	2.1
17	Integration magazine	2.0
18	Random personnel meetings	2.0
Very low to low contribution		
19	Integrated labour terms and conditions	1.9
20	Relocation office	1.9
21	New ways of working	1.9
22	Bonus	1.7
23	Salary increase	1.7

This reinforces our message that a tailor-made approach is needed each time in order to manage the soft side of a business integration project successfully.

In Part III we present a framework using the best practices presented in Part II in order to increase the success rate of integration projects by better managing the soft side of business integration.

PART III: INTEGRATIONAL LEARNING FRAMEWORK FOR MANAGING THE SOFT SIDE

INTRODUCTION

SOFT ISSUES AS KEY FAILURE FACTORS

In earlier sections of the book we identified four key causes for failure of integration processes. These were:

- people problems
- lack of understanding of the acquired company
- lack of a clear purpose or plan for integration
- companies are not compatible

When added together these four soft issues account, in our view, for most of the failures in business integration processes. Recent publications confirm this. As Kets de Vries (1997) indicates, the people aspect, which is critical in every business, is often overlooked.

Sirower (1997) showed that the almost irrational behaviour of those that had to make decisions about mergers and acquisitions caused a lot of integration failures. He also underlined the importance of recognizing the available integration capabilities inside a company. Decisions about takeovers or mergers often seem to be taken with an unfounded optimism explained by synergy beliefs, as discussed in Chapter 3.

Despite careful preparation of a business integration venture, emotions keep playing an important role as Hers (1997) explains. A deal team that has been planning an acquisition becomes excited and wants to close the deal. Calling a deal off often seems very difficult, despite the by now obvious negative consequences in the realization phase.

Davenport (1998) confirms the conclusion that at best half the mergers bring positive results to the shareholders. He also underlines the importance of managing the soft issues for the success of an integration project.

WHAT TO DO WITH THESE SOFT ISSUES?

So: a number of mistakes are made in the area of managing the soft side of business integration. Could these mistakes have been avoided and could the success rate have been improved by doing so? The obvious answer is yes! And yet reality is more complex than this straightforward answer.

The best practices presented in Part II of this chapter are examples of the attempts that the participating companies have made to improve their integration success rate by dealing more effectively with these soft issues. These companies have recognized the importance of managing (some of) these soft issues.

Most of these best practices have been learned the hard way in one or more integration processes. That is, after one or more failures, managers tried to 'do things better' the next time they were confronted with the same problem. This form of learning – from mistakes made in the past – can be seen as learning the hard way. It is not the most cost-effective way to learn. It usually comes at a rather high price in both financial and human terms.

Learning, however, is absolutely necessary if a company wants to improve its business integration track record. The statistics presented earlier show that a failure is much more likely than a success where business integration projects are concerned.

INTEGRATIONAL LEARNING: IMPROVING MANAGEMENT OF THE SOFT SIDE

In order to deal more effectively with these and other integration issues mentioned above, we upgraded our framework for managing business integration: the Business Integration Approach (Figure 5.2).

A critical part of our approach is integration programme management, which we described in Chapter 4. Dealing with the soft-side issues is of course part of the overall integration programme management, but because these soft issues are so often the cause of failure in business integration we decided to make this part more visible in our approach – hence integrational learning. We assume that by improving integrational learning the ability of companies to deal with business integration can be improved, leading to an improvement in the success rate of these ventures.

In the following sections, we will look in more detail at integrational learning. None of the elements of integrational learning presented in the

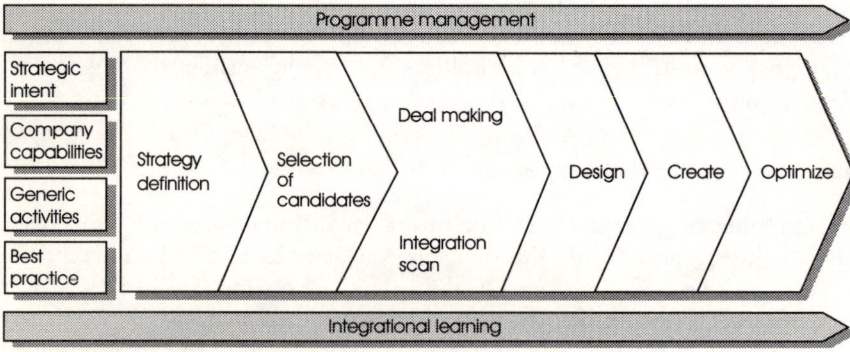

Figure 5.2 The Business Integration Approach.

following sections will be able to ensure the success of an integration project by themselves. Consequently, this presupposes an integrated approach. Integrational learning is only one part, though a very important one, of our holistic Business Integration Approach.

OVERVIEW OF PART III

After the more practical Parts I (Current Practices) and II (Best Practices), we have now come to the part in which we present our framework. This cannot be done without some reference to the theoretical models used as well as to the role that integrational learning plays in our Business Integration Approach.

In Part III we describe what we mean by integrational learning. We also present a further outline of integrational learning in relation to the phases of our Business Integration Approach. This will be done as follows.

In the integrational learning perspective (pp. 151–157), we will present some background focusing on the learning part. We look at managing the soft integration issues as a set of learning processes which require managing if integration is to be effective. This section also contains a definition of integrational learning. Furthermore, we argue the case for a link between organizational development and the personal development of employees as part of our holistic approach.

In the integrational learning areas (pp. 157–166), we will look at the contents of the integrational learning processes. Four different learning areas have been identified. Also, our approach recognizes the difference between the rational and irrational elements of learning, both of which will have to be managed in a successful integration process.

Finally (pp. 166–185), we link best practices, as defined in Part II, with our Business Integration Approach. By doing so, we will provide a practical framework for managing the soft side of business integration projects.

INTEGRATIONAL LEARNING PERSPECTIVE

So, Integrational Learning is about managing the soft side of integration projects. Why do we call it integrational learning? And what do we mean by this?

BACKGROUND IN ORGANIZATIONAL LEARNING

Integrational learning has some of its roots in the organizational learning perspective. DiBella and Nevis (1998) define organizational learning as 'the capacity or processes within an organization to maintain or improve performance based on experience'. They also state that 'learning is about gaining experience, competence building, and avoiding of the repetition of mistakes'.

These definitions clearly indicate that organizational learning is a recurrent process linked to business performance. The core elements of learning, according to DiBella and Nevis (1998) are what we call an integrated or holistic approach, involving top management and a focus which recognizes individual and group learning.

The use of the term 'knowledge' in the following paragraphs should not create confusion. In our view 'knowledge' can be used interchangeably with 'expertise' or 'competence' and refers to the knowledge, skills and attitudes which are part of a company.

A differentiation must be made between explicit knowledge, which is codified and can be made to exist in a physical form, and is therefore directly transferable, and implicit or tacit knowledge, which is not codified and is therefore much more difficult to transfer formally. As Scott-Morgan (1995) has shown, transformation here is handled through socialization.

Learning is a process in which experience is gathered, analysed and transformed into competence, which is used again. The processes that are needed for this transformation will be described in the next section.

CORE LEARNING PROCESSES

Organizational learning consists of a series of four processes which together form an ongoing process or, in the words of Boekhoff *et al.* (1998), the knowledge value chain.

These four core learning processes are:

- acquire or create knowledge
- disseminate knowledge
- apply knowledge
- evaluate knowledge

Each of these processes will be described briefly.

Acquire or create knowledge

These are processes through which a company gathers or creates knowledge. These processes can be externally and/or internally focused. Which knowledge is captured and where depends to a certain extent on factors such as the company's leadership, its strategy, its chosen value discipline, the type of market it operates in, its culture and its employees. There is so much knowledge to gather that selection is always needed; the issue here is what is selected and what is not.

Disseminate knowledge

These are the processes through which a company disseminates (distributes) knowledge. They can be formal, such as an induction course or basic training, or informal, such as the implicit suggestion that something is not done here. Other methods include newsletters, email, special events and telephone conversations. The dissemination of knowledge should lead to competence building inside the organization.

As mentioned, dissemination can take many different forms. If a company wants to ensure effective dissemination, it should control knowledge build-up in such a way that it can be easily disseminated throughout the company and/or its network environment. Formal dissemination, which of course is much more easily controlled, requires the building up of bodies of knowledge (a course, a methodology, a set of procedures etc.).

The impact of the company's culture as well as of the national culture should not be underestimated with regard to the dissemination and later use of knowledge.

Apply knowledge

These are the processes through which acquired knowledge is used by a company in (new) situations.

The availability of knowledge is often not enough to make employees use it; as DiBella and Nevis (1998) point out: 'learning comes at a cost and when that cost is considered too high, what has been learned will not be used'. Remember the smoker, who knows about the dangers of smoking and says he wants to give up smoking, but perceives that breaking the addiction will cause too many problems and therefore continues to smoke.

Or ask newcomers after half a year what they have learned in an organization. Nobody should be surprised to find out that people have informally learned a quite different set of rules than in their formal introduction.

Applying knowledge must lead to changed behaviour if it is to be effective in a company. Talking is not sufficient. In other words, behavioural change is required: avoiding making the same mistakes over and over again through different and more effective behaviour.

Evaluate knowledge

These are the processes through which the value and usefulness of existing knowledge are appraised, and through which are assessed what new knowledge is needed and what knowledge can be discarded. The focus must be on the knowledge as well as on the learning processes, i.e. how do we go about acquiring, disseminating and using knowledge?

LEARNING AND BUSINESS PERFORMANCE

Whether or not (effective) learning will take place depends, according to DiBella and Nevis (1998), on three factors. One is the learning orientation of a company (e.g. is this more process-oriented or more functionally oriented, or more externally or internally focused). The second is whether or not certain facilitating factors are in operation, such as a climate of openness or a culture of continuous education. A third factor involves a combination of certain basic variables, such as an involved leadership (are top managers personally involved in learning?), a systems perspective (what we call an integrated approach) and a learning focus (a balance of individual and team development).

It is assumed that every individual and group will have to go through the learning cycles described earlier, but there will be variations in time, learning content etc.

Like DiBella and Nevis (1998) we would like to underscore the link between learning and business performance. If companies organize their learning well, their business performance will benefit. GE's Six Sigma programme (Lowe, 1998) provides a good example. In our view this requires consistency with the business strategy as well as the business model (including the company culture), as we have argued before.

LEARNING ABOUT INTEGRATION

With regard to business integration, many companies seem to struggle and keep making the same mistakes over and over again. Even in those cases in which a more formal integration approach is available, many basic mistakes are still being made, with the obvious undesired outcomes.

Apparently, knowledge acquisition, as well as the dissemination, application and evaluation of knowledge in business integration, are far from optimal in many companies. What causes can be identified to understand this phenomenon?

Several can be mentioned:

- Lack of experience: not many companies do more than one or two integration projects a year; how many line managers do more than one integration project? So not much experience is being gathered, with the obvious exception of some multinational companies.
- Lack of expertise: when you start an integration venture, not much is known about the complexities of the everyday reality of business integration in a company due to lack of expertise. Unfortunately, practical research has been slow to develop in this area: a lot more attention has been given to the front end, i.e. the making of the deal.

- Lack of methodology: due to the low frequency, it is often seen as not worthwhile to design a company-specific integration methodology, without which it is more difficult to gather, disseminate, apply and effectively evaluate integration management knowledge.
- Lack of evaluation: integration projects are often not adequately evaluated, so that no lessons learned can be gathered. This is easily understood when the failure rate is taken into account: which company wants to discuss publicly an integration failure and the related cost?
- Lack of openness: many mistakes are made and not many companies encourage their managers to present their mistakes (without a negative impact on their careers). By not asking them to do so and to present their recipes for doing it better next time, they reinforce the likelihood of making the same mistake over and over again.
- Lack of recognition: integration projects involve a high level of emotion, which needs to be managed if it is not to hinder the realization of the integration objectives. Managing emotions does not have a high priority in the mind-set of many managers, which complicates the whole process.

INTEGRATIONAL LEARNING: A DEFINITION

At the beginning of this section, we presented four major failure factors for integration processes, all of which are so-called 'soft issues'. Learning about business integration management involves addressing these factors.

This view is supported by what Doz and Hamel (1998) call the learning cycle. They stress that success – of alliances in their case – depends not only on the 'value creation logic ... but also on the effectiveness of each partner's learning about the others and of their joint learning about the environment, the task and the cooperation process of the alliance'.

In an attempt to define learning with regard to business integration, we have introduced the term 'integrational learning' as part of our Business Integration Approach. *Integrational learning* is defined as the set of processes through which a company, its individuals and its groups of employees acquire, disseminate, apply and evaluate knowledge with regard to business integration.

In our view, integrational learning is a dedicated set of learning processes concerned with business integration. It is needed inside any organization that wants to realize business processes like mergers, acquisitions or internal integrations effectively.

Integrational learning is needed to build up and maintain the capabilities for integration management in a company. It is also needed because it deals with business situations in which many facets of the operations change. Furthermore, integrational learning is needed because, due to the high personal impact, emotional reactions will play an important part in these situations. This often results in ineffective behaviour not guided by professional concerns but by uncontrolled personal emotions and anxieties.

CHANGING COMPANIES AND INDIVIDUALS

One of the issues of business integration projects concerns the amount of change for both the companies involved and the employees inside these companies.

Take the case of a merger. Deciding to merge two previously separate companies implies a lot of change at company level. A new vision is needed, possibly underpinned by new values. Adjustments in the client base can or should happen as a consequence of the merger. Sometimes the anti-monopoly authorities may force parts to be sold off in order to avoid market domination by the merged companies.

If the merger really brings synergy, new products may be developed which will have to be put on the market. This will probably be done by changing many elements of the operating model, varying from processes to organizational structures and infrastructure. Culture change will often be needed – the histories of both companies will usually be different. And last, but not least, mergers often reduce the total headcount. Some of the best people might leave, which can cause a serious expertise gap. All these changes at company level can only be successfully realized if the remaining employees change their behaviour.

Working in a different way with new colleagues, who may once have been competitors, requires significant changes in behaviour. Synergy cannot be realized without changed behaviour from the employees of both companies. New teams will have to be formed that must learn to work together based on respect and trust. Achieving cost reductions requires a different way of operating in business processes compared with how things were done before. Many of these changes are not easily realized.

INTEGRATIONAL LEARNING AS THE LINK

Perceived in this way, a successful business integration project is a change project at multiple levels: company, group and individual. In order to handle these company changes effectively, employees should learn about them and use the newly acquired knowledge. According to DiBella and Nevis (1998), this will not be done without a price.

In the case of a merger in which full integration takes place this price can be very high. It definitely implies uncertainty, anxiety, doubt and a decision about whether or not to commit to the new company – in other words, whether or not to renew the psychological contract with the company.

Often this cannot be done based on prior experience and adequate knowledge or capabilities. Integrational learning is therefore needed, because it links corporate (organizational) development with personal development in a strategic framework and a change process context.

As De Geus (1997) states: 'The underlying contract between the company and its members... is that the members will be helped to reach their potential. It is understood that this, at the same time, is in the company's self-interest'. Davenport (1998) also concurs with our approach, which links organizational change with personal development. He too uses the concept of a psychological contract.

Integrational learning, in order to be effective, must recognize both the content and the process aspects. 'Content' refers to what must be learned about business integration in order to be able to perform effectively again in the new (integrated) situation. These content areas will necessarily contain corporate and personal elements. In the next section, Integrational Learning areas, we will discuss the content areas of integrational learning.

'Process' refers to the phasing of business integration, which presupposes a link between corporate and personal change processes, while recognizing the learning cycle discussed before. In the section about managing the soft side we will present an overview of the management of the soft side of business integration.

INTEGRATIONAL LEARNING AREAS

From all the research and experience presented earlier in this chapter, we know that managing the soft factors is critical to success. We have defined four key learning areas, i.e. areas which should play an important role in the learning processes.

Our integrational learning approach recognizes four key areas. These are:

- *Vision learning*: learning about the direction of business (integration). This will provide desperately needed direction in times of serious change, which employees can use to orient themselves and guide their actions.
- *Business model learning*: learning about the changes in markets, clients and all aspects of the ways of working, i.e. about the PMC portfolio and the operating model. Learning how the vision will become reality and how the company will create value for its customers, and by so doing how it will also create value for its shareholders and other stakeholders.

- *Integration process learning*: learning about the way in which the integration objectives will be realized and what the expected impact might be. This will assist employees in guiding their change activities as well as dealing with their own anxieties and other emotions.
- *Individual and group development learning*: learning about how personal and group/team development are related to business integration. This will help employees and groups in managing their own development to align with corporate and personal objectives.

Rational and non-rational

These four components of integrational learning will be introduced in the following sections. Many times before we have referred to the big role that emotions play in business integration. An effective approach for managing these processes will therefore have to address both rational and non-rational aspects.

A simple example illustrates why this is needed. Some time ago, we were involved in consulting for two companies that had announced a merger. The two CEOs had informed the press after consultation with their top managers. As part of our Scan phase, we organized a joint meeting of key managers. During this session it became clear that although all the participants had been given the necessary basic information about the intended merger, many of them did not really 'get it'. Yes, they did know the numbers, but they did not understand the logic behind the merger. Many differences were pointed out and discussed which did not lead to a shared view of the rationale behind the merger. It did not come as a surprise to many that within a few weeks the merger was called off.

This case shows that presenting the rational side of the desired business integration – i.e. the figures that showed more turnover, profit growth and shareholder value – was not sufficient to convince management in both companies of the attractiveness of the merger. It is stressed here that both rational and non-rational elements must be taken into account, as we have argued in Chapter 3. This will be done in the following sections for each of the four areas of integrational learning.

VISION LEARNING

One key component of integrational learning is vision learning, or knowledge acquisition, dissemination, application and evaluation about the mission, business goals and strategy of the company(ies) involved. The strategic direction must be clear if a successful business integration is to take place (see Chapter 3). This refers both to the new company's vision as well as to the integration logic.

Strategic direction

Successfully revising the contract with the company that an employee works for will – on the rational side – at least require an understanding of the strategic direction of the company; what is it trying to achieve? This of course is necessary in order to answer questions like: what am I expected to contribute and how am I supposed to do that?

Therefore a clear mission (statement) will be needed. With the possible exception of internal integration projects, confusion about the mission might come about in many integration processes. In a merger between two companies, top management should make clear what the new company stands for. This should be done in such a way that employees can understand what it means. But this also holds true in acquisitions – even for the acquiring company.

Furthermore, the business objectives for the near future will have to be made clear. What are we trying to achieve over the coming years? How are we going to do this? How does this merger, acquisition or internal integration fit into this framework?

By doing so, top management should also make explicit what the basic values are that are underpinning the new or changed company's mission. These core elements of the company's culture are among the foundation blocks on which the (new) company can be built.

As part of the strategic direction effort, an operationalization of the vision is required in order to guide the design of the product portfolio and the operating model.

Over time, the strategic direction should be reviewed. In certain highly volatile industries no vision can be left untouched over a long period of time. Also, the results of the integration process will have to be taken into account in the process of creating the vision.

Integration objectives and strategy

Besides the business vision, the integration objectives and strategy should be made clear. The integration logic – why is it clear that this integration will add value and should therefore be realized – must be well understood if people are to realize these objectives during the integration process.

Visions tend to be far removed from everyday reality. That is a serious threat to the success of any integration project. If employees are to renew their psychological contract with the company – and we definitely need them to do this in order to achieve the planned objectives – more is needed than just a vision statement.

Attention should be given to reinforcing team spirit and other values that underpin the vision, including the integration part of it. The intended integration benefits should be measured against actual values and prioritized, and this should be communicated.

Communicating the vision

Visions cannot be realized without leadership from people who embody the vision and who present the vision to the stakeholders; people to whom employees can relate and who they can use as role models; leadership that inspires and helps employees to manage their own fears, uncertainties, anxiety, anger, frustrations and other emotions that surface during integration projects.

This is but one of the many leadership challenges in integration processes, as Katzenbach (1997) notes. He identifies challenges such as creating a sense of urgency, defining new performance targets and performing temporary roles during the integration process.

Bringing the vision to the employees is therefore no luxury. It is a bare necessity if employees are to renew their contract with the company and work effectively towards realizing the integration objectives in a new or changed environment. It not only means providing them with the basic facts but also that they should be presented to them by top management. Only these personal presentations will allow employees to re-identify with the company and its leaders. For those who have just been taken over it will be their first meeting with their new leaders. If the latter do not take the time to go and visit their new employees, identification and commitment will be slow to come, if at all.

Organizing road shows or 'town hall' meetings in which top management meet all the employees is one of the means to achieve the integration objectives in this area. Another option is to provide employees and their families with company brochures. In this way, the families of employees will be able to develop an image of the future for their loved ones and of the possible consequences for themselves. This information should of course contain a view of the planned future, including the business integration project in which they are involved.

All these elements require certain capabilities, particularly from top management, but also from the integration management team. Some of them relate to the key role of top management of not only creating the vision but also to communicating it.

BUSINESS MODEL LEARNING

But vision alone is not enough, certainly not in the case of full or partial integration. The second component of integrational learning (or managing the soft side of integration) therefore addresses learning about the changes in the business model, i.e. changes in the product–market combinations portfolio and the operating model.

Markets, clients, products

Employees need to know what the company aims for. To which markets will we sell (and preferably to which clients), and which products and services will we sell? Sometimes only a few changes occur, but more often than not serious changes will be implemented, and these will hurt. Giving up existing clients will be difficult for many sales managers. The same is true of giving up certain markets in order to expand in others. The whys must be clear as well as the hows.

Which products and services will be supplied in the selected markets? Again, sometimes minor changes are implemented in this area. But even then it is important to be clear about this issue.

Next, to clarify the product portfolio, employees need directions about the way in which these services and products will be delivered, i.e. the way in which value will be created for the customer.

According to the framework of Treacy and Wiersema (1995), a clear choice of value discipline will have to be made and communicated. Although some find reality more complex than they do, Treacy and Wiersema presented the need for a clear choice of value discipline in order to avoid getting stuck in the middle. They offered three basic options: product leadership, operational excellence and customer intimacy.

It is important to recognize that changing the way in which value is created for customers creates uncertainty inside a company, because something in which employees have believed for a certain period of time will have to go.

Having operated for many years as a product leader in a local market and then, due to changed market conditions, having to merge to become an operational excellence company is not something that is done overnight. For all the employees to understand, *believe* and practice this requires serious and consistent effort.

Furthermore, the chosen value discipline should be used to guide the design of the operating model. Business integration projects in which more than one value discipline are to be integrated create additional problems that will have to be addressed as part of designing the operating model if business performance is not to suffer during the integration.

Operating model

Clarity about the operating model in all its aspects is required for successful implementation. Changing the operating model often implies many changes that, in order to be effective, will have to be handled in an integrated manner and must be understood in that way.

Changing the operating model involves the following:

- Business processes need to be redefined to meet new targets.
- Organizational structure will be adjusted when two companies fully or partially integrate, for example. Changes in personnel (e.g. headcount reduction) have a serious impact and will have to be made clear. This is also true for the human resource management policies.

- Management systems have to be aligned with business and integration objectives as well as with the value creation paradigm.
- Information technology must be integrated, which often causes many problems.
- Infrastructural change, such as a move to new headquarters, will have a serious impact.
- Culture, although the last aspect, is certainly not the least as far as creating clarity is concerned.

From the standpoint of integrational learning, employees must know about these changes. A number of them can help in bringing about these changes as part of a change or value team, but most employees will not be directly involved and will therefore have to be informed. They will have to acquire the knowledge, skills and attitudes that are part of this operating model change if they are to operate effectively when the implementation takes place. What is more, they will have to believe in these changes if they are to use this new knowledge in their daily operations via their changed behaviour.

Again, rational understanding based on facts is needed. As one of the key failure factors indicates, too often it is assumed that the other entity is understood. Even when the case concerns the takeover of a competitor, it is very risky to assume that one understands the other company. Incompatibility, culturally driven and historically based, is often a cause of failure.

On top of that, understanding of the non-rational element is needed if integrational learning is to take place. Designing a new operating model is a difficult enterprise which requires breaking through the self-evident parts of the current situation in two existing entities. Envisioning what the meaning or the emotional value of the new operating model for various audiences can be is even more difficult, yet is very important.

Another range of capabilities is needed to perform these activities effectively. Not only top management but also integration management need these capabilities. Employees also need to acquire certain capabilities if they are to operate effectively and efficiently in the new operating model.

INTEGRATION PROCESS LEARNING

The third component of integrational learning concerns knowledge of the way in which the integration objectives will be realized and about its impact. How will the integration take place? How quickly? By whom? What does it mean for me? And so on.

Integration processes are change processes of a very complex kind. In many companies they do not happen very often, which implies that deep knowledge about and experience of this type of process are often lacking.

Integration process

Clarity about the integration approach used is needed. This concerns the planning, phasing and control of all change activities – in short, the facts and figures of the planned integration. Without a good integration programme (see Chapter 4) this cannot be given, at least not specifically enough. This will then increase anxiety and stimulate resistance, because people do not know (and understand) what they have to give up for what, let alone when, etc.

Impact

Another key element concerns the impact of the change process and how this will be managed. Here too a planned and controlled approach is needed in order to ensure that employees renew their psychological contract with the company.

Employees should know about the impact of the integration process in all its facets. This implies that they know about the planned changes as early as possible. It also means that their key questions about 'what does it mean for me?' are answered as early and honestly as possible. It also implies that they know about the side-effects and, even more importantly, how to deal with them. Uncertainty is always part of an integration project, but so too can be frustration, anxiety and anger. Recognizing the emotional part of these processes is one precondition for managing them, and that is something that concerns everybody involved.

Knowing about these phenomena and how to manage them is critical in effective integration management, yet this is certainly not enough on its own. It also means understanding the phenomena, and more importantly acquiring skills to manage the side-effects. The integration teams should have know-how in these areas, but the company should also give employees the right kinds of support for dealing with these aspects of integration.

In Part II of this chapter, some best practices for this part of business integration were described. However, not many are yet available, and certainly not in those companies that do only a few acquisitions a year without sharing a corporate framework and experience.

Effective integration implementation depends to a very large extent on this component of integrational learning. For integration to become reality the employees involved will have to know about the new vision and the new business architecture, what they require of them and how they will be put into place.

Communication

That is why communication is at the heart of every integration project. Communication is very important because it is a vehicle for informing (telling) the employees involved about the why and the how – or, in short, for acquiring and disseminating knowledge. Even then, the participants in our research concluded that there is never enough communication. And they are right.

As part of the integration programme a communication plan will have to be developed in order to achieve effective internal and external communication with all stakeholders. For the media used we refer to Part I of this chapter, where an overview of the possible media was presented. The need for dedicated communications media is underscored here as well as the need to monitor the effectiveness of the communication media.

Change management capabilities

Capabilities for dealing with an integration process and its impact are badly needed yet not often available. Managing insecurity, anxiety and stress are – as we said before – part of this. Hence telling people about the facts and figures without educating them in the other areas is quite ineffective.

Creating flexibility and the willingness to bridge (cultural) gaps is also necessary to ensure future cooperation. People must be helped to give up their current roles and behaviours and acquire new ones. Resistance management is part of this.

Therefore integrational learning is about stimulating employees and motivating them for change, and facilitating their self-motivation is also part of this. This again implies knowing and understanding the integration process and its impact as well as learning to deal with these aspects adequately.

INDIVIDUAL AND GROUP DEVELOPMENT LEARNING

Successful integration requires not only new information or even new knowledge but also changed behaviour from the employees involved. In other words, this involves a full learning circle, from knowledge acquisition to knowledge dissemination, application and evaluation. Managing an integration process therefore also implies that these learning cycles can be run effectively and efficiently.

As DiBella and Nevis (1998) point out, different learning styles exist inside companies. They use the following categories of learning styles: correction (learn from own operations and use knowledge for incremental improvements), innovation (learn from own operations and use knowledge to make transformations), adaptation (learn from external sources to make incremental changes) and acquisition (learn from external sources and transform own operations with it).

Recognizing these and other learning styles, we agree with Dibella and Nevis (1998) that a company can use several learning styles and that no learning style *per se* is better than any other. It is the match between strategic intent, internal capabilities and integrational learning that defines which learning styles are adequate in an integration project.

Integrational learning, in our view, will take place at the level of the individual as well as at group level. Therefore the final integrational learning component is about ensuring that knowledge acquisition, dissemination, application and evaluation can take place as part of our holistic integration approach.

One of the core objectives here is to build trust. Trust is a complex phenomenon, which is of great value during the realization. Trust is not something that happens overnight. It requires confirmation in behaviour. It takes time to grow and is something that can grow between individuals, but it must be broadened to groups and companies if a merger between two companies is to be successful.

Trust can be seen as the 'glue that binds people together as they work in ambiguous, uncertain environments in ambiguous, uncertain times. It is also at the root of a leader's credibility or lack thereof', as Harari (1997) writes. He argues that trust must be part of the operating model of a company. He is quite clear about the trust issue being an 'either/or'. In his view there is not much grey between the black and white.

Talking about trust in a company is one thing; creating trust in two companies that are becoming one is a different ball game. And yet, trust is an absolute necessity if the integration project is to succeed. Therefore integrational learning must address this issue effectively.

Individual development

How the division between individual and group learning is made depends on the qualities of the company(ies) involved. It is certain, though, that the basic capability development and deployment will always be based on individuals. Successful integration projects therefore provide individual employees with the means necessary to develop themselves, aligned with the corporate development. For example, these can be part of the services offered by a development centre or part of a change management programme.

Group learning

On top of the individual development, all groups that are involved in the integration process will have to go through a learning process as well. Where a team approach is adopted in one or more groups this becomes critical.

In our view, successful integration will almost always mean joint efforts from individuals in new groups to achieve targets. The following groups can be identified:

- CEO(s) and top management
- M&A team
- integration team
- line management

- staff management
- Works Council
- employees

Each group will have to go through its own learning cycle, which will vary in duration as well as in content. The starting point will also differ: because of the nature of these activities the CEO and top management will be involved at the start, whereas staff management and employees will be involved later in the integration process.

An integration project can be seen from this learning perspective as a unique opportunity to organize a management or employee development programme. Because of its horizon, not many projects offer such development opportunities to those who want to experience all the elements of a management role.

INTEGRATIONAL LEARNING: MANAGING THE SOFT SIDE – AN OVERVIEW

Managing the soft side of business integration projects is a complex and compelling challenge. As we have shown, it starts long before the actual deal is done or the final decision to integrate two parts of one company is made.

In our view, integrational learning will help to manage the soft side of business integration effectively. First of all, because of the linking of learning with business objectives, integrational learning helps to deliver the desired integration results.

Because it addresses all the people-related aspects of business integration, integrational learning is the vehicle for managing the soft side issues; see also the integrational learning areas: vision, business model, integration process and individual and group learning.

Furthermore, as a set of learning processes integrational learning – when applied effectively – results in an approach that can be applied and evaluated in a company. Its recurring character permits adaptation to changing circumstances, new people, new strategies and policies etc.

Finally, because it recognizes the various learning levels – company, group, individual – it facilitates management at those levels in an integrated way. And that is just what is needed to improve business integration projects.

In the following sections, we have linked a number of best practices defined by the managers involved in our project with our integrational learning framework. This has resulted in further elaboration of our framework.

We will briefly discuss the phasing and the related best practices, where we will focus on phases 3 to 6.

INTEGRATIONAL LEARNING (1): STRATEGY DEFINITION

Very often strategy definition takes place as an independently recurring process, the outcomes of which should be revisited as part of the business integration venture. In Chapter 3 we have already provided a framework for strategic decision making. Here we will look at some of the building blocks that to a large extent define the quality of integrational learning.

Clarity of the vision

Looking at the four areas of integrational learning, it becomes clear that clarity of the vision is a prerequisite for integrational learning to take place. What is it that we are trying to realize? How easy is it to understand? Is the vision available throughout the company and understood by its employees?

Shared vision

Another important element is the level of alignment of top management with regard to the vision. Do they really see this as their vision, or is it forced upon them by the CEO? Despite the fact that nowadays macho CEO behaviour is usually seen as counter-productive, in reality this still will be the case in many companies.

Clear business objectives

No vision can be fully agreed to without a clear translation into measurable objectives, not only in financial terms but also in a broader format such as the business balanced scorecard, which also recognizes customers, internal processes and innovation as key areas.

These objectives are definitely needed if integrational learning is to take place. They guide all endeavours in the area of business integration because they are the ultimate testing grounds in which integration strategies can be defined and individual cases validated.

Align the portfolio with the vision

Decision making with regard to business integration presupposes a clearly aligned portfolio of markets, clients and services. A vision without translation into these areas is too vague to use in business integration. It is also needed so that employees can understand what the impact of the vision on today's world is. In highly volatile markets there can be no misunderstanding of the desired clients, market shares, supplied services etc., or of the way in which value is created for clients.

Align the operating model

A clear translation of the vision into an operating model facilitates integrational learning because this is the final part of understanding the vision and the way in which it must be realized.

Table 5.9 Best practices in the Strategy definition phase.

Integrational learning areas	Strategy definition phase
Vision	❍ Define a clear vision ❍ Agree to a shared vision ❍ Define clear business objectives
Business model	❍ Align portfolio(s) ❍ Align the operating model ❍ Agree the Business Integration Approach
Integration process and impact	❍ NA
Individual and group learning	❍ Agree a knowledge management policy

Agree the Business Integration Approach

As part of the building-up of integration knowledge, it is very important that a company defines its Business Integration Approach. This should preferably be done independently of a specific case, using all the available knowledge about this area in the company.

By defining its own approach the company not only provides itself with a framework for managing business integration projects, but also provides the basic framework for learning in this area.

Agree a knowledge management policy

An effective vision nowadays requires a clear knowledge management policy. Each company needs to make clear how it and its employees will ensure further development of the available knowledge. This provides another starting point for integrational learning.

Table 5.9 presents an overview of the integrational learning areas and best practices that apply to this phase of our Business Integration Approach.

INTEGRATIONAL LEARNING (2): SELECTION OF CANDIDATES

The next phase of our model addresses integrational learning in the selection of candidates. This process almost always presents difficulties, which, if they are not effectively dealt with, may seriously affect the remaining phases. We are now in a new mode: one or more candidates are available and the process is under way.

Agree the selection criteria

Reconfirmation of the criteria that will be used with all the stakeholders involved in this part of the process is no luxury. Clarity about these criteria is required for integrational learning to take place effectively.

Table 5.10 Best practices in the Candidate selection phase.

Integrational learning areas	Candidate selection phase
Vision	❍ Agree selection criteria
Business model	❍ NA
Integration process and impact	❍ Confirm phasing
Individual and group learning	❍ NA

Confirm phasing

The same is true for the phasing of this project. Assuming that some integration objectives have been defined and communicated to those involved in this part of the project, integrational learning requires clarity regarding the phases and steps that will be taken. In other words, effective integration programme management must be implemented.

Table 5.10 summarizes the best practices in this phase.

MANAGING THE SOFT SIDE (3): THE SCAN AND DEAL-MAKING PHASE

One of the key lessons from past experience is that integration management starts long before the actual deal is made. A number of activities must be performed in order to ensure that effective integration (whatever the required level) can take place, once it has been decided that a sound deal or decision can be made. That is why this phase runs parallel to a number of deal-making activities and ends with the final deal or decision making itself.

The main objectives of the Scan phase are to support the decision-making process. Managing the soft side in this phase is done in various ways:

- ❍ assess the 'soft elements' of the current situation of the companies or units involved
- ❍ appoint top management
- ❍ set up integration management
- ❍ define the outline of thc planned integration
- ❍ assess the integration capabilities at both ends
- ❍ assess the feasibility of the planned integration from the soft side
- ❍ ensure top management alignment
- ❍ announce the decision

Assess the 'soft elements' of the current situation of the companies or units involved

Taking the wrong decision was one of the major failure factors in business integration projects. In Chapter 3 we outlined the need to improve the quality of the decision-making process. Furthermore, earlier in the book we underlined that the lack of understanding of the other company is one of the major failure factors,

From the integrational learning perspective, the due diligence process should include a number of activities focused on the assessment of current non-financial aspects. One is a vision assessment, in order to understand the long-term direction alignment. Another has to do with assessing the PMC portfolio and value discipline and the possible differences between both companies.

In addition, assessing the operating models will help to understand options for integration and possible integration benefits. Too often mistakes have been made because it was assumed that one understood the operating model specifics of the other company.

Furthermore, using the integrational learning perspective underlines the need for a more detailed assessment of the present cultures, because the culture failure factor is by now very unpleasant. Also, an assessment of the terms and conditions is important, since these very often determine cost to a large extent.

Appoint top management

Top management should be in the driving seat as early as possible. No deal should be signed without agreement from those responsible for the defined outcomes (business and integration objectives). The deal should therefore be linked to management contracts with top management.

Early appointment of top management (in this phase) has another advantage. They can play a role in the assessment of all aspects of the company to be acquired or to be merged with.

Set up integration management

Not only should top management be appointed, but also the managers responsible for integration. In the case of an acquisition this is usually an appointment at the acquiring company. Ideally, however, this is done by managers from both companies.

This appointment also serves several purposes. One is the participation of those responsible for actually managing the integration at an early stage. They will have to agree – before the deal is done – that the planned integration is feasible.

Define the outline for the planned integration

Another very important contribution is the design of the outline of the integration programme. Approving this outline should be part of the decision-making process. The lack of an integration plan has too often caused too much harm and led to underestimating the feasibility, cost and duration of integration.

Assess the integration capabilities at both ends

Although mergers, acquisitions and internal integrations are very popular these days, not many companies seem to have the necessary capabilities for these projects. Assessing the available integration capabilities at both companies is necessary in relation to the desired level of integration. Full integration without the availability of qualified management is a no-go in our view. In deciding who should be appointed, it should be remembered that running an ongoing business is definitely something different from managing an integration process.

Assess feasibility of the planned integration from the soft side

As a contribution to the deal-making process, an in-depth assessment of the feasibility of all the human aspects should be performed. Too often, lack of mutual understanding has been the reason for a failed integration. Once (part of the) preferred top management has been identified, personal chemistry can be tested. Cultural assessment should provide clues here as well as informal meetings. Recognizing gut feeling (not as the guiding factor, but as an important indicator of possible issues) and dealing effectively with it (validating it as much as possible) plays a key role here.

Ensure top management alignment

Although this is clearly an activity in the deal-making process, the future top management and certainly integration management should ensure that there is real alignment in the Board that is making the decision with regard to the deal. Too often we have seen that after one of the directors, who was keen on the acquisition, left the company an acquired company was left in limbo because nobody wanted to get involved and get his or her hands dirty.

Announce the decision

Most CEOs will be eager to announce the deal just made, especially in the case of a 'fancy' acquisition or merger. In the event of an internal integration some of them might be less tempted, because this is not often seen as an important step forward. Announcing the decision is the first public act with regard to the planned integration and must be carefully planned and worded. This announcement can create much anxiety and fear. A clear vision should be presented to all stakeholders in order to give them a chance to understand what is really meant by this planned integration.

This communication should be the first step of a larger communication effort, which will be more detailed in the next phase. The top management of the new entity and integration management should be involved to ensure that the right message is sent to all stakeholders.

Table 5.11 Best practices in the Scan phase.

Integrational learning areas	Scan phase
Vision	❍ Assess vision(s) ❍ Agree vision ❍ Define clear integration objectives ❍ Ensure top management alignment
Business model	❍ Assess portfolio(s) ❍ Assess operating model's: ❑ business processes ❑ organization ❑ management systems ❑ employees and capabilities ❑ culture ❑ information technology ❑ infrastructure ❍ Appoint top management
Integration process and impact	❍ Assess feasibility ❍ Set up integration management ❍ Agree outline integration programme ❍ Involve Works Council ❍ Define outline communication plan ❍ Announce deal/integration decision
Individual and group learning	❍ Assess integration capabilities ❍ Link organizational and personal development

Table 5.11 presents an overview of the integrational learning areas and the best practices, defined in Part II of this chapter, that apply to this phase of our Business Integration Approach.

MANAGING THE SOFT SIDE (4): DESIGN PHASE

Once the decision has been made to integrate two or more units, or once the deal is made, the next phase can start. This is what we call the plan phase. Formal procedures with government authorities, Brussels DG IV etc. will take a certain period of time. Yet this time can be used to plan as much as possible for the start of the integration implementation.

One element of managing the soft side will become very important, especially if the companies involved will have to wait for a formal green light for their intended integration, and that is trust. If this is lacking, this waiting period might be nothing else, because no joint development will be done. But ideally, this period should be used for shared planning of the realization of the intended integration. Mutual trust and understanding are needed for this. What and how much is shared, certainly between former competitors, cannot be said in advance. A very careful process is needed to handle this delicate situation, which might still lead to going back to being competitors again.

This phase focuses on the design of the business model for the integrated entity. The first step in this phase is to define a detailed integration programme, including the integrational learning activities and the extension of the integration management organization.

The main objectives of the Design phase are to plan the integration process in detail and design the new entity in all its aspects. Managing the soft side in this phase is done in various ways:

- communicate the vision
- appoint the joint integration management organization
- design the integration programme, including the communication plan
- develop integration capabilities at both ends
- design the soft elements of the business model in relation to the hard parts
- start the information exchange and integration meetings
- inform stakeholders
- motivate employees
- design change education

Communicate the vision

A successful start to the planning phase of an integration project requires a joint understanding by all those involved in planning the driving force or vision that lies behind this effort. All those involved should be informed by top management and integration management what vision they want to realize and what they see as the key integration objectives, benefits and hurdles.

The vision should be presented in joint sessions, where those to be involved in the planning process can participate. Ensuring their understanding of the vision is the starting point for adequate planning. One part of this concerns the prioritization of the integration objectives. This will be needed to detail the integration programme.

This must be supported by checking whether or not 'the message' has been understood. All the effort that is put into this at the front end of the integration project will pay itself back twice because early discovery of misunderstanding, doubts, uncertainties etc. will help to deal with these problems. If this is not done effectively, these hindrances can take many different forms later in the process and are then much more difficult to deal with.

Appoint the joint integration management organization

The first step in the Design phase should be the appointment of a joint integration management organization according to the outline agreed in the Scan/Deal-making phase. The use of profiles will help to ensure that all the necessary capabilities are on board before the venture really gets off the ground.

All of the companies or units involved in the integration process should be represented in this integration organization. In addition, the availability of functional expertise in one form or another is important. Critical to the functioning of this integration organization is the quality of the integration management team. If too much diversity is hindering the team at the beginning, an independent outsider can help manage the team process to ensure that progress is made in all aspects and not only in output terms.

Involve talented employees

One of the key issues in managing the soft side of integration is the retention of key employees. Among the ways to ensure that they stay are asking them to participate in the integration organization or appointing them to the new top management team.

Future managers can be asked to guide value teams to redesign the operating model for their units. By doing so, continuity between design and realization is ensured, which will enhance success.

Detail the integration programme

Another step is the development of an integration programme that aligns with the integration objectives. The input to this step is the integration outline that was agreed in the previous phase, i.e. the Scan/Deal-making phase.

This is part of the programme management activities, but it is mentioned here because the actual joint development is an important part of the integrational learning approach advocated by us.

Design the communication plan

Designing a full communication plan is part of the effort required to develop an integration programme. Using the communication outline from the Scan/Deal-making phase, developing a full-blown communication plan, and detailing the stakeholders, the media used, the communicators and the timing will be absolutely necessary.

We refer to Parts I and II of this chapter, where details of the design of all communication activities were presented.

Develop integration capabilities at both ends

Based on the integration capability assessment performed in the Scan/Deal-making phase, a development plan might be needed in this area. If that is the case, high priority should be given to ensuring that the entire integration organization can make use of sufficient capabilities. This can be done in various ways, such as the integration programme organization developing its own capabilities, involving qualified colleagues, and hiring external integration management consultants. Again, this investment will have a very short payback period.

Once this is done, a further development of integration capabilities might be planned for those parts of the organization that will become involved in the next phase. This could be part of the possible change education planned for the preparation of the Create phase.

Design the soft elements of the business model in relation to the hard parts

In this phase, many projects and activities will be focused on the design of the changes in the product portfolio and operating model.

From the management of the soft side point of view, special attention should be given to the 'me issues' (headcount reduction, appointment policy, terms and conditions), but also to culture and new ways of working. Uncertainty is unavoidable during transformations such as integration projects, but the period during which these 'me first' issues are unanswered should be as short as possible.

Outflow management

Outflow management starts with a clear decision about how many and who will have to go. A difficult issue in the event of a merger is having to deal with two candidates for every job available. This requires creative solutions, some of which – such as offering other positions inside the company – might be more easily realized in big multinational companies than in smaller ones.

Handling the outflow of employees is important, not only for legal reasons but primarily because it significantly affects the position of the company in society and its remaining employees. Techniques for managing this, as presented in Part I of this chapter, can be helpful in managing this issue. A decent social plan is, of course, part of this.

Appointment policy

A second issue has to do with clarity regarding the appointment policy for the new entity. Employees should know as soon as possible how the (remaining) positions will be filled. Both procedures and qualifications should be carefully developed in this phase so that in the Create phase this process can take place as quickly as possible.

Compensation package

A third and very complex issue has to do with terms and conditions for contracting employees (also called benefits and compensations). As soon as possible a decision has to be made regarding the handling of this issue.

The key questions concern replacing the existing different sets of terms and conditions by one new set for all employees involved. The answer is often not an easy one and should certainly be answered in outline during the Scan/Deal-making phase because of the high cost of these decisions.

The new company management should have a clear explanation of how they will handle this, now and in the future. What will happen to new employees that join the company in one or two years' time? And what does integration mean when new colleagues who do the same job earn more than others do? As pointed out in Part I of this chapter, there are also national boundaries to take into consideration, as well as related legal contexts.

Finally, the impact of current compensation systems on the willingness to change cannot be underestimated. Too often, these systems lag behind and support a historic rather than a desired way of working. Deciding on how to reward change-support behaviour is not a luxury, but something that needs careful consideration, even in those situations where it has been decided to maintain different compensation systems next to each other.

Part of this decision will already have found its way into the management contracts that top management will have signed as part of their appointment to their new jobs. Integration managers could also be rewarded in this way. For other employees consistency with the integration programme is important.

Culture

Based on the outcome of the culture assessment, the defined vision and the selected value discipline, a definition of the desired culture has to be developed in this phase. This cannot be done effectively without understanding the 'unwritten rules of the game' mentioned by Peter Scott-Morgan (1995). Another important check is consistency between culture and other elements of the operating model and the chosen value discipline.

New ways of working

Experience teaches us that telling employees that they *must* work differently now does not work. As argued before (pp. 149–166), more is needed here. Redesigning the operating model (e.g. transforming it from a functional organization into a process organization as part of the move towards operational excellence) also requires the design of knowledge dissemination methods. This must ensure that employees not only know, but understand and will apply these new ways of working.

Inform stakeholders

In the Design phase, not only will the communication plan be further developed but communication with the stakeholders will also be continued. How far this can be taken depends on the dependency on a 'green light' from government officials. As long as the final go-ahead has not been given, communication with (external) stakeholders will have to wait or be minimal.

This Design phase will be used to prepare communication materials for external stakeholders. For internal stakeholders, a dedicated newsletter in which they are informed about the progress of the integration project is one of many media that might be designed. This should be published in this phase.

Motivate remaining employees

Although most employees will not see much happening in this phase, they know about the plans for integration and many of them will be anxious, especially in those cases where the headcount will be reduced.

From the integrational learning perspective it is important that employees are told by top management about the vision, the plans and the implementation. Either at the end of the Design phase or at the beginning of the Create phase, employees should be presented with the vision and the plans. This is the first part of the framework for them to decide on their future commitment to the company. In the Create phase more detailed information will be given to them to provide a more complete picture of what will happen, what it means for them and what they can and should do to help realize the integration objectives.

Motivating employees will help them to stay and recommit themselves. This can be done in a number of ways. Management behaviour is one key factor in this. From the moment that management announces an integration, they will be watched to see what they really mean, i.e. what they do to ensure that integration can take place. The most carefully planned communication efforts cannot mask management behaviour from which employees can deduce that a planned business integration is not very important. If the top is not seen as sharing the integration vision and participating in it, employees will know that this is not a high-priority item, so motivating them for integration will be much more difficult.

Increasing pay could be considered as one of the means of motivation, but its effectiveness must be doubted in many cases. Planning a number of integration events is certainly needed when a big integration project is to succeed, but more informal information exchange should be also planned at this stage, as well as integration meetings.

Design change education

Although most companies nowadays understand that the implementation of a new information system requires user training if they are to operate it effectively, for various reasons this view has not yet often been transferred to integration projects.

Table 5.12 Best practices in the Design phase.

Integrational learning areas	Design phase
Vision	○ Communicate vision ❑ Prioritize integration benefits actions ❑ Present company information ❑ Organize top and integration management explanation ❑ Hold joint presentations ❑ Check message reception
Business model	○ Refine portfolio ○ Define new operating model ❑ present unwritten rules ❑ define appointment policy ❑ design new ways of working ○ Decide on terms and conditions
Integration process and impact	○ Appoint joint integration organization ○ Involve talented personnel ○ Detail the integration programme ○ Finalize communication plan ○ Define outflow management including social plan ○ Set up mobility office ○ Perform communication to stakeholders ❑ Organize get-to-know meetings ❑ Publish integration magazine ❑ Communicate progress ○ Hold personnel survey ○ Plan motivation of remaining employees
Individual and group learning	○ Design change education ○ Develop integration capabilities ○ Design BI/MD programme

If the employees involved in the integration process are to operate effectively and efficiently (which is important given that so many integration projects focus on cost reduction), they should be able to. Time and again, due to unclear integration programmes and uncertainty, employees operate ineffectively and inefficiently. They focus almost all of their activities on the inside of the company and by so doing lose sight of the customer. This provides a good opportunity for competitors to win a number of customers.

Effective and efficient behaviour can be proactively stimulated by training a number of key employees (or change agents) in managing the change processes involved in integration, and by educating many employees about the planned effort, their involvement, the related uncertainties and the impact on their professional life. For many broad cultural differences, it will pay to design a programme to handle these in advance and make employees aware of what could happen and how they can prevent or handle these complex situations.

If employees learn about the developmental opportunities linked to an integration project, this might help them to operate more effectively instead of becoming resistant due to their own anxieties.

In the plan phase all these design activities will have to be performed before the actual implementation of the integration can start.

Table 5.12 provides an overview of the integrational learning areas and the best practices, defined in Part II of this chapter, that apply to this phase of our Business Integration Approach.

INTEGRATIONAL LEARNING (5): CREATE PHASE

Once the preparations have been completed and all the designs are available, the integration process leaves the drawing board and becomes reality for many employees. In this phase – which we call 'Create' because a new situation is created – the new entity becomes reality. This can only be done by ensuring that a basic level of integration is realized.

This is usually a period of profound change and will therefore have to be as short as possible. The often mentioned '100 days' could be seen to apply to both the Design and Create phases of our approach, but a word of caution is needed here. Although the case for speedy Design and Create phases seems to be clear-cut for Anglo-Saxon companies, this is not automatically true for other cultures, such as South European cultures. Careful consideration from cultural and feasibility perspectives is needed in the Plan phase when the duration of the Create phase is decided upon.

The main objectives of the Create phase are to operationalize the integration process according to the agreed integration programme and achieve a basic level of integration. Managing the soft side in this phase is done in various ways:

- share the detailed vision
- inform employees about 'me issues'
- perform change education
- implement operational model design
- perform two-way communication
- motivate employees
- monitor integration programme realization

Share the detailed vision

Integrational learning processes consist of the creation (in the Design phase), dissemination, use and evaluation of knowledge. These processes will play a role in this phase, with dissemination being the most important.

Now that the vision has been detailed during the Design phase, employees will have to be informed about the outcomes. Again, this is very important if they are to act effectively in the new situation. Therefore presentations are needed as well as written material to support the detailed vision. The link with the new or changed business model should be made very explicit, so that middle management in the organization can internalize these views and use them in their guidance of other employees during this and the final phase of the integration.

Inform employees about 'me issues'

The beginning of this phase will consist furthermore of informing employees about the 'me issues' as was planned in the previous phase. This will take a lot of effort if many employees are to go. This should be handled first before any other employee related actions are taken.

Perform change education

The planned change education should take place as early as possible in this phase so that maximum use can be made of it by the employees involved. This should help employees to recommit and must be seen as one of the many means of focusing management attention on the remaining employees.

Implement operational model design

This is the phase in which the actual headcount reduction is realized. Individual employees will be told and will make their arrangements. Active outflow management is a prerequisite for effective handling of the large numbers of employees that will have to leave.

It is also the time to appoint employees to new positions according to defined procedures. Ensuring that individuals get all the support that they need in deciding where to go to (which job to apply for inside the company, or participation in job rotation), or even to look elsewhere, is very important.

By providing a support agency, the company can help to improve the quality of the decision-making process that individual employees will have to go through. This will also help to deal effectively with the large number of practical questions regarding moving, pensions, salary abroad etc.

This is also the phase in which compensation systems have to be changed, if it has been decided to do so in the planning phase. This will take considerable effort and cannot be completed in a short period of time.

Also, the implementation of managing cultural differences will have to start in this phase, otherwise misunderstandings might easily arise and create unnecessary problems and delays.

Perform two-way communication

Communication efforts directed at internal stakeholders will take place as described above and in other ways, such as newsletters, bulletin boards, posters and logos.

It is critical in this phase that a number of meetings are organized between integration programme management and employees in which personal contact is possible and many questions can be answered.

Another method is to organize feedback workshops in which randomly selected employees inform top management and integration management about their views on the progress of the integration project.

Site visits and other informal meetings and special events will further help employees to get to know their new colleagues better and learn to work with them.

Motivate employees

There are many ways to motivate employees, as well as to demotivate them. We have already discussed the importance of management behaviour.

In complex change processes, a simulation might be a very attractive option to learn about the new working situation even before it actually starts. As De Caluwe (1997) has described, simulations are a very powerful instrument for dealing with complex changes. They help employees to learn more effectively and by doing so speed up the implementation of the integration.

Monitor integration programme realization

Integration programme management will have to include monitoring the soft sides. Without tracking progress in these areas, problems will arise which will hinder the planned realization. This also implies that progress will be monitored whether or not knowledge dissemination and application take place. If the latter is the case, additional interventions must be implemented to ensure that the integration objectives can be realized.

Table 5.13 presents an overview of the integrational learning areas and best practices, defined in Part II of this chapter, that apply to this phase of our Business Integration Approach.

INTEGRATIONAL LEARNING (6): OPTIMIZE

After the basis for integration has been laid, fine-tuning can begin. This is another taxing challenge because the full benefits of integration must be

Table 5.13 Best practices in the Create phase.

Integrational learning areas	Create phase
Vision	❍ Communicate detailed vision ❑ Perform road show by top management ❑ Hold joint presentations ❑ Underline team spirit ❍ Present company information ❍ Demonstrate new behaviour
Business model	❍ Implement operating model changes ❑ new ways of working ❑ manage cultural differences ❑ adapt terms and conditions ❍ Demonstrate new behaviour ❍ Reward new behaviour ❍ Implement job rotation
Integration process and impact	❍ Inform employees about 'me issues' ❍ Organize team building ❍ Ensure re-identification with company ❍ Perform two-way communication ❑ Communicate progress ❑ Implement relocation office ❑ Hold feedback workshops ❑ Organize get-to-know meetings ❑ Organize informal meetings/events ❍ Motivate employees ❍ Monitor programme realization (soft side)
Individual and group learning	❍ Realize change education ❍ Train in new ways of working ❍ Train for new jobs ❍ Link company and personal development

ensured in this phase, assuming that external and internal circumstances allow this.

The main objectives of the Optimize phase are to fully achieve the planned integration objectives by optimizing the PMC portfolio and operating model.

Managing the soft side in this phase is done in various ways:

❍ review the vision and communicate
❍ optimize the understanding of the PMC portfolio
❍ optimize the use of the operating model

- ❍ inform stakeholders about progress and results
- ❍ perform employee survey
- ❍ monitor integration programme realization
- ❍ close down the integration programme

Review the vision and communicate

In this last phase, employees should learn about whether the company is still on track with regard to the vision and/or whether this needs adaptation due to external or internal circumstances. Employees also need to know this if they are to behave effectively.

Part of this concerns the decision about whether or not to change the integration objectives, based on newly gathered insight into the performance of the company(ies) in relation to the market. Changing the desired integration benefits requires careful communication and might even lead to additional integration training effort.

Optimize the understanding of the PMC portfolio

It pays to validate in this phase whether or not knowledge about the desired PMC portfolio has been shared and understood, and whether or not employees act according to the value discipline selected. If not fully realized, new interventions need to be defined and performed in order to ensure that the desired optimization will take place.

Optimize the use of the operating model

The same is true for application of the operating model knowledge that has been shared out in the Create phase. Once the basics are in place, more effective management systems can be implemented. These in turn will help to stimulate change in the operational behaviour of individuals and groups of employees.

The management of cultural differences remains an important consideration. In this last phase the decision will have to be made about whether or not additional post-integration programme cultural activities will be needed to ensure favourable development of the company culture.

Inform stakeholders about progress and results

The information flow to external and internal stakeholders should continue up to the end of the Optimize phase. This should be stimulating for employees. For example, if operational excellence has been chosen, which will be demonstrated to clients by using certain performance scores, it will be important to demonstrate this not only to clients but also to employees. In this way their success in realizing the business integration can become measurable and, if applicable, remunerable.

Perform employee survey

As part of the close-down of this phase and as part of the evaluation effort, an employee survey could be used in order to gather as much information about the implementation as possible. This information should be used in making the final decision about closing down the integration programme and whether or not post-integration programme activities are needed. It can also be used to improve the business integration methodology by using these experiences to upgrade this approach.

Monitor integration programme realization

Integration programme management will have to include monitoring the soft sides. If progress in these areas is not tracked, problems will arise which will hinder the planned realization. This also implies that you should monitor whether or not knowledge dissemination, application and evaluation take place. If the latter is the case, additional interventions will have to be implemented to ensure that the integration objectives can be realized.

Close down the integration programme

As the last part of the Optimize phase, the integration programme will be closed down at a certain time. Here we want to stress that this close-down also implies that the integration organization is dismantled. The close-down should be celebrated, assuming that successful realization of the integration objectives has taken place.

Table 5.14 presents an overview the integrational learning areas and best practices, defined in Part II of this chapter, that apply to this phase of our Business Integration Approach.

CONCLUSION: MANAGING THE SOFT SIDE

In this chapter we have presented a number of practices related to the management of the soft side of integration. This third part has focused on presenting a framework for integrational learning within which this management can take place.

We have argued that a learning approach is useful in trying to come to grips with the majority of the failure factors of business integration projects. The integrational learning perspective as part of our Business Integration Approach will help to manage business integration projects much more effectively because of its more holistic approach. By doing so, the impact of these failure factors can be reduced and the management of these projects can become more effective.

Table 5.14 Best practices in the Optimize phase.

Integrational learning areas	Optimize phase
Vision	❍ Revise vision ❍ Communicate integration benefits
Business model	❍ Exchange best practice ❍ Optimize operating model changes ❑ new ways of working ❑ manage cultural differences ❑ adapt terms and conditions ❍ Perform employee survey
Integration process and impact	❍ Motivate ❍ Upgrade team ❍ Hold personnel survey ❍ Communicate progress ❍ Monitor programme realization ❍ Mark end of project
Individual and group learning	❍ Evaluate project ❍ Update company Business Integration Approach

6
MANAGING FOR SUCCESS

❖

INTRODUCTION

Remember Servico and Gersco? Are you wondering how their story, as told in Chapter 1, would have turned out if they had applied a business integration approach? We can only guess, but in the next section we revisit the Servico–Gersco case and look at what a more professional way of handling this venture might have looked like.

The final section looks at changing markets and technology and their impact on value-creation strategies. These new ways of creating value for clients create new integration needs. Integrational learning can and must, in our view, play a key role in these developments.

SERVICO AND GERSCO REVISITED

Could the case of Servico and Gersco – as described in Chapter 1 – have been different? Of course, but the case definitely needs a lot of changes.

SERVICO BUSINESS STRATEGY DEVELOPS

Imagine again the successful British service company Servico, with a long tradition in the UK of supplying quality services to various British market sectors. Over time the founders of Servico have made place for new management and the company has grown.

The Board of Servico has regularly commissioned extensive market and client research to identify new trends in their key market sectors and used the outcomes to adjust their corporate strategy. They have decided that they need to make a step change and must start to play a role in European markets. They also decided to go for growth via acquisition. Autonomous growth was too slow to accommodate their quickly changing clients' needs properly.

Servico defined an acquisition strategy which was agreed by the Board and commissioned a search for potentially interesting companies that would fit the profile and criteria they had defined. All of this was based on a shared view of key market trends, among which Europeanization was one. The corporate finance consultants they hired presented a list of candidates, which was carefully screened.

A short list of five companies (among which was Gersco) in three different European countries were considered to be qualifying candidates. Several representatives of the Board of Servico together with their consultants visited all the candidates. All companies made presentations and tried to get a first impression of the other party.

Then the team of consultants, which consisted of corporate finance specialists and business integration consultants, organized a careful selection process in which the short list of five was reduced to two, with which negotiations would start.

GERSCO DECIDES ABOUT ITS FUTURE

During the same period Gersco management was discussing its future. The president/owner had indicated his desire to sell the company because of his private circumstances. Gersco management discussed the issue openly and looked at possible future strategies. Although the owner was willing to sell the company to the managers, they considered that this was not the most attractive option. They looked into various scenarios and decided – based on market and client research – that they needed further expansion quickly, and especially a presence in other European countries.

The experience that they had had with European networks was not favourable. The current management thought that it would be better to find a parent from abroad which would work alongside the existing management. This would not only increase their European presence but would also solve the problem of the investment necessary for further growth.

Once they had clarified the criteria they would use in selecting a possible partner or investor, they started to look for one. This process took about a year before they found several serious and interesting candidates, one of which was Servico.

In the past Gersco had had some bad experiences in finding candidates for mergers and acquisitions. Their attempts to grow in Germany had led to several acquisitions, at least one of which had turned out to be at best a partial failure. Therefore, despite attractive financial offers from certain companies, they kept on looking until they found a company which also fit the other criteria (soft factors) that they had defined.

DEAL-MAKING

When the expectations of parties were met in the initial talks, they decided to proceed to the deal-making process. Servico was concerned to make the right choice in selecting a foreign company. Therefore, the Servico Board wanted a careful fit analysis to be performed with Gersco as soon as possible.

A team of Servico managers – including several candidates for the position of becoming one of the future managers of Gersco as well as the intended integration manager – and integration consultants performed a scan in all Gersco locations. Furthermore, the Gersco management was also invited to set up a team which could visit some of the Servico sites to do the same fit analyses, but now from their own perspective. This team was supported by integration consultants.

Soon the issues about the different ways of working between the various locations of Gersco became known. Also, the issue of language was raised during the kick-off of the fit analysis activities. Functional meetings – e.g. between sales reps of Servico and Gersco – took place to look into these processes and assess how cooperation could take place and what problems would need to be solved.

In this way, the fit analyses looked at all the components of the business model of both companies. A list of issues was made by both analysis teams, which they presented to each other. Together, they presented the outcomes to a joint meeting of the Board of Servico and the Management Team of Gersco.

Based on these presentations, a decision was made to go ahead with the planned integration and the analysis teams were asked to develop an integration plan outline together, given a set of clear objectives. This was done, and the team proposed a phased partial integration and developed an outline plan for this. A careful consultation process took place which made it possible for Servico to make a specific offer that not only included financial elements but also an integration implementation outline that was quite specific.

A separate team of managers, using the outcomes of the analyses, developed a failure scenario for the Servico Board. The Gersco Management Team was asked to do so as well. These were also inputs for the decision making that took place in this phase. This helped to keep the downsides in mind and to keep the process balanced.

The negotiations were concluded positively and a realistic deal was made that satisfied the parties involved. By ensuring the participation of current Gersco management and by involving a Servico manager in the Gersco Management Team as well as a clever earn-out scheme, the parties were confident that a sound foundation was laid for a successful business integration.

The Gersco Management Team was modified. The president/owner became an advisor and relations director to the Management Team. One

Servico manager joined the Gersco Management Team and became responsible for Finance and ICT.

All managers at Gersco and those managers at Servico involved in the integration signed a management contract that was based on the integration targets and the integration plan outline. An integration budget was approved as part of the overall deal.

To celebrate the deal, a North Sea ferry was hired and many of the employees of both companies met their counterparts on a – thankfully quiet – North Sea. A big party was organized which led to many discoveries, including a mutual liking for certain food and drinks.

WORKING TOGETHER: THE SECOND STAGE

As part of the implementation a large-scale communication effort to all the stakeholders involved resulted in almost no loss of clients and many positive reactions from the involved employees in both Servico and Gersco. From day one the written communications were bilingual (English and German) despite the agreement that the company language was to be English. All managers were given a brief workshop in cultural diversity between the English and the Germans and how to deal with those differences. They were trained to make their staff aware of the existing differences and similarities. They in turn worked with their personnel as part of the communication effort to deal with these issues.

Employees at Gersco were also given the opportunity to buy shares in their own company. After a number of years these shares could be converted into Servico shares once the decision was made to do so.

A joint integration team was set up to design the new business model for Gersco and identify the adjustments needed in the Servico business model. A number of business processes, the organization, ICT, management systems etc. were redesigned to accommodate the international cooperation. The organization of Servico was also improved. A 100 days approach was used to define an integration programme, based on the objectives and the decision to go for partial integration.

The issues identified in the pre-deal phase were looked at more closely and solutions were proposed. A joint Servico–Gersco Integration Steering Group managed the whole effort in this phase and controlled the budget allocated for the realization.

In this period several new issues arose. One was caused by a market problem which led a number of clients of both Servico and Gersco to temporarily reduce their demand for services. Initially, both companies reacted in their 'traditional' ways, i.e. by optimizing their own situations. This was quickly signalled by the joint Integration Steering Group, which discussed the issue and proposed a joint solution to both the Gersco Management Team and the Servico Board, which after some consideration accepted this joint solution to the market problems.

Another issue arose in the Gersco Management Team regarding the Frankfurt–Berlin relationship. Because the Gersco integration manager and a Servico manager had been on the Gersco Management Team since the deal was made, the issue could be handled there. The former owner also played his part because he was still involved in Gersco and would remain so for the next two years.

One of the more successful elements in the integration programme was the management exchange programme that was put in place. The joint redesign of the business model as well as this exchange programme greatly increased mutual understanding and helped to implement new ways of working together. Learning from each other was institutionalized in this way. This was only a small part of the knowledge management that was put in place in the first 100 days.

CREATING NEW BUSINESS MODELS

At first, quite a few of the Servico staff thought that their German colleagues were going to work according to the Servico standards because Servico had taken over Gersco. They soon learned from a number of communications that this was not to be the case. Instead, the acquisition was the opportunity to upgrade the business model of each company by learning together as much as possible and putting best practice into place. They had to work together before they could realize this.

So, after the 100 days of design and planning were over, many employees were involved in learning new ways of operating. Where this was feasible, training was given to mixed groups of both Servico and Gersco employees. Of course, email and the Servico–Gersco intranet helped the employees of both companies to communicate in many ways. Not many employees left, and those who were challenged to play a crucial role in this integration venture stayed and did their bit to make it a success.

After some time it became clear that despite the careful planning a larger budget was needed for training employees. The use of new technology and learning from each other had stimulated individual development among the employees of both companies. This investment was, however, certainly not wasted. Performance showed a positive development after a while. One of the more difficult moments came when Germany played against England in the European Football Championship. Old sentiments were resurrected and led to some unfriendly communications. The German team won, but after some time, this incident was soon forgotten, especially when through joint efforts several new clients were added to the client list.

THE FUTURE

Both companies consider this business integration venture to have been a success, because a number of the integration targets have been met. Not all of the objectives were realized. Setting up a joint management development programme contributed to realizing a joint learning process across both companies, based not on obligation but on a drive to improve and to excel together and by so doing beat the competition. This leaves plenty of operational issues to be dealt with. However, the learning has resulted not only in a sharing of knowledge but also of the underlying values and especially trust. And that helped.

'BEYOND' INTEGRATIONAL LEARNING

Integration is here to stay, but the type of integration will change. Part of that change is caused by changing business strategies as a reaction to changing markets. Other changes come from changing value creation strategies. In this final section we outline some of these changes and the expected impact they will have.

The need for an integrated approach to business integration will not decline. On the contrary, in these new value-creation strategies in particular a joint Business Integration Approach is needed. Strategic decision making remains one of the key elements here, as well as integration programme management. However, we will focus on the one element that is so often responsible for failure and thus also for success: managing the soft side.

CHANGING MARKETS

The final decades of the 20th century saw an increasing number of acquisitions, internal integrations and (mega-)mergers. This process has not yet come to a halt. In the years to come the Americas, Europe and the Asia Pacific region will continue to experience these phenomena. The result of this movement towards 'larger and bigger' can be easily predicted: fewer and larger conglomerates.

It will be clear that this cannot go on indefinitely. Failed mergers or acquisitions will limit the life cycle of those conglomerates that cannot realize the desired benefits of integration, both in cost and growth terms. But changing market conditions may also lead to reconsideration of the size of these conglomerates.

Splitting up may become an attractive alternative if this strategy is carefully selected and implemented, such as the ICI and Zeneca demerger. A forced split-up usually turns out to be very expensive and a damaging experience from which some companies never really recover; some even disappear once it happens.

Splitting up, as a carefully chosen strategy, will not mean that those companies that merged or were acquired will be divided along the original lines. On the contrary, we expect different split-ups depending on the value-creation strategies that are chosen.

At the same time the world has seen the rise of companies which were not there even two years ago, and which in that time have grown to become significant players in their markets. Speed is characteristic of these companies: both speed of development and speed in terms of time to market. E-business in particular offers many opportunities for setting up new businesses and designing new operating models including new and significantly different ways of working.

CHANGING VALUE CREATION STRATEGIES

As is becoming more and more clear, business success in many areas depends on choosing the 'right' strategic direction without having all the necessary information, and implementing this as quickly as possible. In other words: speed and agility are vital.

The changing strategic roles of companies can be seen everywhere. The way in which companies create value for their clients can change dramatically in a short period of time. This must be understood against the background of a growing realization of the importance of the value chains or networks of which a company is part.

The importance of the interdependence of businesses and clients was nicely illustrated in the last couple of years of the twentieth century in preparing for the millennium. Many businesses recognized then the need to really look into their supplier and client network and verify where any possible problems could arise due to the millennium bug in software used by themselves, their clients and their suppliers which would threaten their own operations.

Once recognized, these value networks provide opportunities for growth and development, especially when new network technology such as the Internet is recognized in its facilitating and renewing role. In other words, there are new options for creating value.

In their book about value disciplines, Treacy and Wiersema (1995) presented three ways of excelling in creating value for clients for an individual company: to excel by the constant delivery of new products (Product Leadership); to excel by offering the best quality–price balance (Operational Excellence); and to excel by giving customers all that they need (Customer Intimacy). Nowadays we need a wider perspective, such as that of the value network and the various roles that can be played in that network.

A business can excel in creating value by concentrating on a specific part of a value network, such as manufacturing or distribution. Where many companies so far have designed, manufactured and sold their products themselves, often including the after-sales services, many can now be seen to be concentrating on only one or two of these aspects. Nike has outsourced the production of its shoes for years. IKEA does the same with the manufacturing of its furniture. Many airlines still fly people from A to B, but the food on the planes is provided by other specialized companies and the baggage is handled by third parties.

The outsourcing of some business processes can be done while the company itself maintains control over the whole value chain to certain customers. This is proving less and less common. Moreover, there is a move towards organizing a value chain or network with several companies where each contributes to the whole by playing a specific role.

One company, for example, might concentrate on playing the role of organizer of the whole value network (value chain). This really changes the relationship. Squeezing the supplier for the last penny is not helpful in this situation. Drastic changes in supplier–client relationships must be made if this new way of working together is to be successful. Another company might focus entirely on the customer end of the value network and manage the servicing of certain groups of clients using their well-known brands. For example, supermarkets are introducing financial products to their service offerings, while at the same time outsourcing their previously-owned factories which produce their food products. The interdependence of these networks is evident, while control is being shared.

And of course there are companies which try to become industry leaders by setting an example. Microsoft is often mentioned in this category. This, however, could change if other companies go for this role. Those companies, however small they may be at the start, that can quickly design and implement new e-business concepts will become leaders in their industries.

THE IMPACT OF CHANGING VALUE-CREATION STRATEGIES AND INTEGRATIONAL LEARNING

These exciting new strategies cannot be implemented without having a significant impact on a company's business model. Not only must the relationships with clients and suppliers be revised, but many of the other aspects of current operating models will need to change. And that is where integrational learning becomes crucial.

What does integrational learning have to do with these market, technology and business strategy developments? As we have shown in Chapter 5, the key aim of integrational learning is to link business or corporate development with individual development. And that is what we come across again in these developments.

Realizing a network strategy is yet another form of business integration (into the value network), and this must be made to work. We are convinced that the same mechanisms are at work here as in mergers, for example, and that, if companies do not learn from the mistakes made with mergers, acquisitions and internal integrations, they will not be able to benefit from a network strategy.

From our point of view this implies the following:

Vision learning

Each of the above-mentioned value network strategies is clearly revolutionary in its recognition of the mutual dependence of companies and clients. Instead of seeing this only as a threat, it is welcomed as an opportunity to develop a company further. This development, however, will be quite different because the value creation paradigm has changed significantly from the one used before. This implies that vision learning is an absolute must if the people involved are to understand what is really meant and needs to be realized.

If a company gives up its manufacturing and concentrates, for instance, solely on the servicing of certain customer groups through its brands, it will create havoc inside the organization. Employees will have to be able to 'learn' this strategy if they are to realize it effectively. This definitely implies a change of vision and certain values.

A value network-based strategy is not something that can be developed in a 'traditional' business strategy development process. If, thanks to earlier integration activities, a vision learning process has been implemented, this will help to further develop new strategies. This process will involve many more people than just those at the top of the organization. If speed and agility are vital, the strategy is made while it is being worked on and implemented, as part of the clear direction in which the company moves. This in itself is a continuous and critical learning process.

Leadership plays a key role in this, not only by setting an example, but also by providing the opportunity for as many people as possible to participate in vision learning processes and by doing so contributing to the development and realization of new business strategies. Two-way communication is another key to realization.

Business model learning

The paradigm shift in the relationship with suppliers cannot be sufficiently underlined. Moving from a relationship driven by 'the lowest cost for us' to joint profit-maximizing cooperation affects all aspects of the existing business models, at both the supplier and client ends.

However, this can only be done effectively if the value network as a whole is clearly understood. The relationship with clients, for instance, might change dramatically in the case of a company which will focus only on manufacturing. This implies new clients, a different portfolio of products and different markets.

Only if this is clearly understood can the optimization of the operating model take place. The design and realization is clearly a learning process which involves all employees to a greater or lesser extent. As we explained in Chapter 5, this learning should address both rational and non-rational elements.

Integration process learning

The third component of integrational learning addresses the way in which the new business (value network-based) strategy and related operating model will be implemented. As is the case in mergers and acquisitions, clarity about the steps to take and the measures that need to be in place to track progress in the realization is absolutely essential.

In particular, when a significant paradigm shift is taking place, careful programme management will be needed to manage the transition. Questions such as 'When will we stop having a supplier–client relationship and start with the new partnership?' need to be clearly answered if the venture is to succeed. This change will become more continuous due to the volatility in many markets. Careful management of the underlying learning processes is therefore considered a significant strategic contribution.

Individual and group learning

This is a not just a change in the organizational chart but a drastic change in the way that a company works, which can only be realized if employees acquire the required knowledge, skills and attitude. Changing employee behaviour is vital, as is changing group behaviour in order to rid the company of behaviour that used to be required (squeezing suppliers) and develop new behaviour (working together, sharing knowledge), looking at the whole network and not just 'our' company.

This learning is critical in order to succeed in volatile markets, which will remain volatile and thus will keep demanding changes in both products and services and the way in which these are delivered.

INTEGRATIONAL LEARNING AND NETWORK VALUE STRATEGIES

Not all companies will go for a network-based strategy, but those that do will realize that their business integration history plays a critical role in implementing these new strategies.

This book has focused on managing business integration ventures more effectively in order to achieve a company's business and integration objectives. Despite the current high failure rate, we are convinced that business integration ventures can help companies in the realization of their vision and strategy.

We are also convinced of the developmental value of these situations for employees. If business integration is no longer just another word for downsizing and simple cost reduction, it definitely offers significant opportunities for both companies and employees in their desire to grow in a changing and demanding environment.

If both employees and companies learn to manage these developmental processes, guided by their visions, business integration offers many developmental options and by so doing offers options for the fulfilment of basic corporate and human needs. It is our obligation to manage these towards much higher success rates than are currently achieved. By developing integrational learning capabilities, a company will not only increase the success rate of its mergers, acquisitions or internal integrations, but will also increase its ability to deal more effectively with changing client demands, changing markets and changing environments.

BIBLIOGRAPHY

Anslinger, P. L. and Copeland, T. E. (1996). Growth through acquisitions: a fresh look. *Harvard Business Review*, Jan–Feb.

Ansoff, H. I. (1968). *Corporate Strategy: an Analytical Approach to Business Policy for Growth and Expansion*. John Wiley & Sons, New York.

Bakker, J. C., Helmink, J. W. A. and Platschorre, J. L. (1998). *Realizing Successful Business Integration*. Twynstra Management Consultants, Amersfoort.

Boekhoff, T. *et al.* (1998) *Managing the Knowledge Factor.* Twynstra Management Consultants, Amersfoort.

Caluwe, L. de (1997). *Veranderen Moet Je Leren*. Den Haag

Collins, J. C. and Porras, J. I. (1994). *Built to Last: Successful Habits of Visionary Companies.* HarperBusiness, New York.

Davenport, T. O. (1998). The integration challenge. *Management Review*, January, pp. 25–28.

DiBella, A. J. and Nevis, E. C. (1998). *How Organizations Learn*. Jossey-Bass, San Francisco.

Doz, Y. L. and Hamel, G. (1998). *Alliance Advantage: the Art of Creating Value.* Harvard Business School Press, Boston.

Drucker, P. F. (1992). *Managing for the Future.* Butterworth-Heinemann, Oxford.

Geus, A. de (1997). *The Living Company.* Harvard Business School Press, Boston.

Goold, M. and Campbell, A. (1998). Desperately seeking strategy. *Harvard Business Review*, Sep–Oct, 131–143.

Hammond, J. S., Keeney, R. L., and Raiffa, H. (1998). The hidden traps in decision making. *Harvard Business Review*, Sep–Oct, 47–58.

Harari, O. (1997). Curing the M&A madness. *Management Review*, July/August.

Harari, O. (1999). The trust factor. *Management Review*, January, pp. 28–31.

Hers, F. (1997). Overnemen en dan toch kleiner worden. *FEM*, 13 December, 38–39.

Janis, I. K. (1971). Groupthink. *Psychology Today*, November.

Katzenbach, J. R. (1997). The myth of the top management team. *Harvard Business Review*, Nov–Dec, 83–91.

Kets de Vries, M. (1997). Interview with Manfred Kets de Vries by Frank de Graaf. *FEM*, 18 January, 56–57.

Lajoux, A. Reed (1997). *The Art of M&A Integration: a Guide to Merging Resources, Processes and Responsibilities.* McGraw-Hill, New York.

Lowe, J. C. (1998). *Jack Welch Speaks: Wisdom from the World's Greatest Business Leader.* John Wiley & Sons, New York.

Marks, M. L. and Mirvis, P. H. (1998). *Joining Forces: Making One Plus One Equal Three in Mergers, Acquisitions and Alliances.* Jossey-Bass, San Francisco, CA.

Nevis, E. C., Lancourt, J. and Vassallo, H. G. (1996). *Intentional Revolutions: a Seven-Point Strategy for Transforming Organizations.* Jossey-Bass, San Francisco.

Palepu, K. (1996). *Presentation SMI Meeting 1996.* Harvard Business School, Boston, MA.

Scott-Morgan, P. (1994). *The Unwritten Rules of the Game.* McGraw-Hill, New York.

Sirower, M. (1997). *The Synergy Trap.* The Free Press, New York.

Treacy, M. and Wiersema, F. (1995). *The Discipline of Market Leaders.* Addison-Wesley, Reading, MA.

Wijnen, G. (1994). *Programmamanagement.* Twynstra Management Consultants, Amersfoort.

INDEX

❖